D0812482

Richard the Lionheart

Richard the Lionheart
THE MIGHTY CRUSADER

David Miller

WEIDENFELD & NICOLSON

Weidenfeld & Nicolson

The Orion Publishing Group Ltd
Orion House, 5 Upper Saint Martin's Lane, London WC2H 9EA

British Library Cataloguing-in-Publication Data
A catalogue record for this book is available from the British Library

General Editor Julian Thompson

ISBN 0-297-84713-9

Distributed in the United States by
Sterling Publishing Co. Inc., 387 Park Avenue South, New York, NY 10016-8810

Cartography and diagrams by Peter Harper
Design by Gwyn Lewis

Printed and bound in Great Britain by Butler & Tanner Ltd, Frome and London

Contents

List of Maps and Illustrations

Editor's Foreword

Steven Runciman, in his three volume history of the Crusades, calls Richard the Lionheart 'a bad son, a bad husband and a bad king, but a gallant and splendid soldier'. Amin Malouf, the author of *The Crusades Through Arab Eyes*, is less complimentary:

> The 33-year-old red-headed giant who wore the English crown was the prototype of the belligerent and flighty knight whose noble ideals did little to conceal his baffling brutality and complete lack of scruples.

Any study of Richard I of England undertaken in the early twenty-first century risks being burdened with two sets of 'baggage'. The first is the habit of judging historical characters and their actions by the standards of affluent, influential (in the opinion-forming sense), liberal (with a small 'l') western society; actually, a minority of the global population. Second, the campaign for which Richard is best known, the Third Crusade, was one of a series of expeditions over nearly four centuries (1095–1464) which have become the object of censure, especially, and not surprisingly, in the Arab and Muslim world, but also elsewhere. So much so, that in 2001 President Bush caused a flutter in the dovecotes of political correctness by alluding to the war against terrorism as a crusade.

It is arguable that this condemnation is special pleading and ignores the fact that invasion and the seizure of other people's land was not exclusive to western European Christian armies. Palestine, Egypt and Syria had been invaded countless times throughout history, as a cursory study of the Old Testament shows. At the time of the Crusades, the Arabs (or Saracens as they were called) and Seljuk Turks were merely the most recent arrivals. As with the invasions carried out by their co-religionists further afield – for example, the Moors in Spain, and later the Mughals in India – however advanced their civilisation and sophisticated their lifestyle, these invasions were established, and then sustained, by force. As Stephen Runciman has pointed out, 'Unlike Christianity which preached a peace that it never achieved, Islam unashamedly came with a sword'. Bringing enlightenment to barbarians, infidels or heretics (the classification depending of course on the point of view of the beholder) at the point of a sword, latterly the bayonet, has been used as an excuse for aggression since the dawn of history, by representatives of almost every race and religion. The Crusaders were neither the first nor the last in the history of humankind to go to war for this reason.

Richard has attracted criticism for allowing the massacre of some two to three thousand prisoners (the exact figure can never be established) after the fall of Acre. In modern times, this is seen as a disgraceful episode. But we should not judge it by twenty-first century standards, rather by those of the twelfth century. Saladin ordered the execution of every Templar knight captured at the Battle of Hattin, which had preceded Richard's arrival in the Holy Land. A hundred years later, the *beau sabreur*, Bertrand du Guesclin of France, massacred English prisoners on two occasions. Henry V had his French prisoners killed during the final moments of the Battle of Agincourt. In 1396, the Marshal of France ordered the dispatch of some 1,000 prisoners on the eve of the Battle of Nicopolis, so that the army would be spared the bother of guarding them when battle was joined. As David Miller points out, in the long term the Saracens bore Richard no ill will for the massacre.

Our aim is to examine whether or not Richard I was a great commander. So the need to justify the Crusades in moral terms, along with charges that Richard failed in his filial, marital and regal duties, can be set aside; there is in those matters no case to answer as far as this study is concerned. What we want to know is, put simply, was Richard any good at the three levels of warfare: tactical, operational and strategic? How competent was he as the commander of a multinational force? Was he a true professional meeting the precept attributed to Field Marshal Slim, 'amateurs talk tactics, professionals talk logistics'? In this assessment, David Miller brings a soldier's eye and experience to the study of Richard in his campaign against the Saracens, led by the equally legendary Saladin.

Tactically, Richard was never wrong-footed. He had that great gift of being able to 'read' a battle, like a good scrum-half can 'read' a game of rugby. This enabled him to seize the opportunity when it presented itself. When that moment arrived he was almost always out in front, leading and inspiring. Nowhere was this more evident than at Jaffa.

His handling of all arms (cavalry, infantry, archers, siege artillery and ships) was deft and sure, and marks him as a great tactician. This and his speed of reaction reminds one of the skill of a first-class panzer grenadier divisional commander of the Second World War. At the operational level, his handling of an army, and his command and control of up to five different national contingents and many minor ones, was exceptionally good.

Strategically, he campaigned successfully thousands of miles from

England and France, his home bases, dependent on a sea line of communication, yet without any of the disasters experienced by earlier and later commanders in similar situations, who were often operating far closer to home. Much of this success was due to his planning and logistical skills. The terrain in which Richard was campaigning was arid and devoid of food stocks for men and horses. Even water was in short supply, and what was available was often unusable after the Saracens had poisoned the wells. Richard's marches were carefully planned and, whenever possible, coordinated with his fleet to provide flank protection and supply. He even arranged for a laundry organisation to keep his soldiers' clothes clean. David Miller has rightly dwelt in detail on the logistics of armies at the time – a subject that is too often ignored, or misunderstood. Richard was a student of military science, and especially the Roman Flavius Vegetius Renatus, and carried a copy of his book, *De Re Militari*, with him on campaign.

One could argue that all this military expertise is irrelevant. Richard failed to achieve his objective and that of the Third Crusade: recapturing Jerusalem. After his second attempt at marching to besiege the city, with Saladin retiring before him, destroying crops and poisoning wells, he halted at Beit-Nuba and reluctantly concluded that he could not risk his army by besieging Jerusalem. Even if he captured the city, it was highly unlikely that it could have been held by the Crusader army. Not only would many of the commanders and soldiers have left, with, in their eyes, their task completed, but Richard himself was under pressure to leave, to return to England where his brother John was treasonably negotiating with the King of France. Before he withdrew from Beit-Nuba, Richard was able to make up his logistic shortages by capturing a large supply caravan after a night reconnaissance patrol which, typically, he led personally.

Richard never attained the objective of the Third Crusade, but nor was he defeated in the field, and his achievements were considerable. When Richard arrived in Palestine, Saladin controlled nearly the whole of what had been the Kingdom of Jerusalem, and most important, the coastline, except for a small strip of land occupied by the Crusaders besieging Acre. At this point, Saladin was well on the way to realising his aim of ejecting all Westerners from the region, and his army had enjoyed a run of successes. He and his army were coming to be seen as invincible, rather in the manner of Rommel and the Afrika Corps seven and a half centuries later. When Richard left Palestine a three-year truce had been agreed, and the Crusaders had regained control of most of the coast. He had successfully commanded a multinational coalition force in most trying circumstances, complicated by the fact that the leaders of the larger contingents within the army – proud and independent-minded dukes, princes and kings – were bent on pursuing their own ends, which often ran contrary to each other.

Seen with the benefit of hindsight, Richard was correct to withdraw and not attempt siege operations at Jerusalem. Wellington was once asked what he deemed the test of a good general. He replied: 'To know when to retreat; and to dare to do it.' Richard was more than a good general. He was, to use an expression coined by Montgomery, 'a general grand chef'.

Julian Thompson

Acknowledgements

It is inevitable in a book such as this that the author will have received help, advice and encouragement from a wide variety of people. I had a particular problem with the research into horses and received invaluable help from two sources. The first was the King's Troop Royal Horse Artillery, where Captain Edward Botteril and Lance-Bombardier Sam Butterworth went to a great deal of trouble to find information by locating references to nineteenth-century horse handling and feeding. The second was a one-time colleague and distinguished former commanding officer of the 17th/21st Lancers, Lieutenant Colonel Reggie Purbrick, who found time in his new home in South Africa to advise on the transportation of horses, a subject in which he has great expertise.

Professor John Gillingham, a distinguished scholar of the period, gave me advice, as did Professor John Pryor, who has unrivalled expertise of twelfth-century shipping in the Mediterranean. Finally, but by no means least, my good friend Robert Hall gave constant encouragement and proof read several chapters for me.

I would also like to thank the staffs of the London Library and of the Prince Consort's Library in Aldershot, who, as always, were ever ready to help.

I convey my thanks to all of the above, but the responsibility for the facts, views and opinions expressed in the book is mine alone.

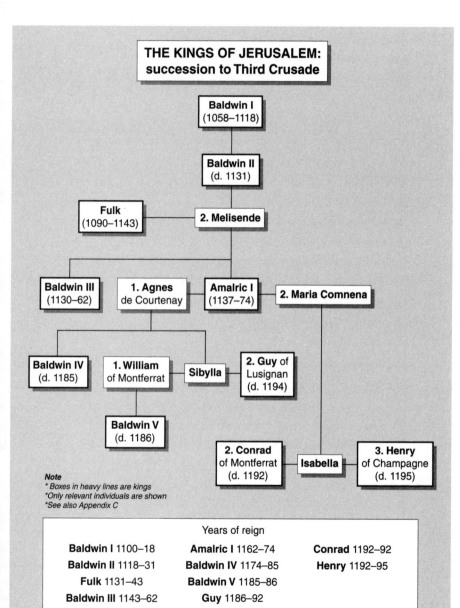

THE KINGS OF JERUSALEM:
succession to Third Crusade

Baldwin I
(1058–1118)

Baldwin II
(d. 1131)

Fulk
(1090–1143) — 2. Melisende

Baldwin III
(1130–62)

1. Agnes
de Courtenay

Amalric I
(1137–74) — 2. Maria Comnena

Baldwin IV
(d. 1185)

1. William
of Montferrat — Sibylla — 2. Guy of
Lusignan
(d. 1194)

Baldwin V
(d. 1186)

2. Conrad
of Montferrat
(d. 1192) — Isabella — 3. Henry
of Champagne
(d. 1195)

Note
* Boxes in heavy lines are kings
*Only relevant individuals are shown
*See also Appendix C

Years of reign

Baldwin I 1100–18	Amalric I 1162–74	Conrad 1192–92
Baldwin II 1118–31	Baldwin IV 1174–85	Henry 1192–95
Fulk 1131–43	Baldwin V 1185–86	
Baldwin III 1143–62	Guy 1186–92	

Introduction

If ever there was a man born to be a soldier, it was King Richard I of England, commonly known as 'The Lionheart' – virtually his entire adult life was devoted to fighting in a succession of wars and against a wide variety of enemies. His reputation as a warrior is secure, but as a general his name is always associated with an apparent military failure – the Third Crusade. This book examines Richard I as a military commander in the context of that campaign, covering the period from the start of his preparations in 1189 until his departure from the Holy Land in October 1192.

Richard was a controversial character as a king, as a person and as a husband, but this book concentrates on his ability and performance as a military commander. Political issues are also examined, since these were a continuing problem throughout the Third Crusade and they repeatedly diverted Richard's attention from military matters. The details of Richard's personal life, however, are of no concern here; what matters for a general is whether his soldiers will follow him and that he wins battles, or, at the very least, that he does not lose the war, and that is how Richard will be judged.

Richard was born on 8 September 1157, the third of five sons of King Henry II Plantagenet (1133–89) and of his redoubtable wife, Queen Eleanor (1122–1204). Henry was a man of unbounded energy who, through a mixture of fighting and diplomacy, created a great kingdom, which included England and a greater area of France than that ruled by the King of France. In 1152 Henry, then aged nineteen, married Eleanor, Duchess of Aquitaine, who had only recently had her marriage to King Louis II of France annulled. She was eleven years older than her new husband, but a woman of exceptional talents, abilities and determination. Two years later Henry was crowned King of England and Eleanor became the only woman ever to have been queen of both France and England. Eleanor retained a passionate interest in her native Aquitaine, and she intended from very early in his childhood that Richard would inherit the duchy; as a result he was brought up in the Aquitaine tradition and spoke French rather than English throughout his life. As part of this plan, Richard was created Duke of Aquitaine at the age of fourteen and soon began a military career that was to continue until his death in 1199. He fought in a rebellion against his father in 1173–4, but was pardoned and subsequently had his father's support in suppressing a revolt in Aquitaine.

Henry II's eldest son, William, died in infancy, and his second son, Henry, died in 1183, leaving Richard as the heir to the English crown. Henry II had declared a desire to go to the Holy Land, although without any known intention of actually doing so. When the news of the disastrous Crusader defeat at the Battle of the Horns of Hattin reached Europe in the late summer of 1187 Richard, always eager for adventure, was the first prince in northern Europe to take the Cross. It was not, however, until he succeeded his father in 1189 that he had the political, financial and military resources necessary to mount a Crusade on the scale he knew to be necessary.

Richard was a complicated man. He was tall, good looking and had bright red hair, all of which he inherited from his formidable mother, together with her undoubted courage, her charm, and her love of music. Given his privileged background and upbringing, he was somewhat self-willed and had a very violent temper – an inheritance from his father – which could be triggered by seemingly trivial events. His energy and speed of travel were such that he was reputed to be able to fly and, as these pages will show, he was a man whose personal courage and leader-ship in hand-to-hand fighting were beyond dispute. Indeed, he threw himself with great enthusiasm into any fight or skirmish, and the greater the odds against him, the more he seemed to enjoy it. On a few occasions, one or other of his own men advised him to observe greater caution, but this usually earned them a cutting rebuke, and having delivered it, the king went ahead anyway. Even Saladin, the great Saracen leader, and Richard's most redoubtable foe, remarked in a discussion with the Bishop of Salisbury after the Third Crusade was over, that Richard was foolishly imprudent 'in thrusting himself so frequently into great danger'.

One aspect of Richard's time on crusade that needs to be placed in perspective, is the frequency with which he was taken ill. He was cer-tainly very unwell shortly after arriving in Acre, but was by no means alone in that. Indeed, the Queen of Jerusalem died there several months before Richard's arrival, together with her two daughters, and some time later so too did the Count of Flanders and Friedrich von Schwaben, the leader of the German Crusaders after the death (by drowning) of his father. Other notables to die of illness in the course of the Crusade in-cluded the Duke of Burgundy, who expired only a few days prior to his departure on the homeward voyage. Even though King Philip of France was only in the Holy Land for just over a month he, too, was taken ill, losing all his hair and fingernails. It may well be that Richard suffered from the same ailment as Philip, but that his superb strength and physical fitness pulled him through more rapidly and effectively. On the other side, Bahā' al-Dīn Ibn Shaddād makes frequent mention of Saladin and other senior Saracens being sick. It is possible, therefore, that Richard was sick no more frequently than any other Crusader, but that the illnesses of lesser mortals were simply not worth recording.

Richard possessed almost all the knightly virtues – humility being a notable absentee – but beyond that he was a thinking man, who was as knowledgeable about warfare as any commander of his day, his only equal in that respect being his arch-rival, Saladin. But, although his extensive campaigning obviously had something to do with this, Richard was also a student of military science and, in particular, of the Roman Flavius Vegetius Renatus (Vegetius), carrying a copy of his book, *De Re Militari*, with him wherever he went. This author and his book are discussed in more detail in Appendix A.

In order to give some idea of how Richard spoke and expressed his thoughts, extracts from letters he wrote and reports of remarks he made are given in Appendix B. The latter are, of course, second- and third-hand, and are in English rather than the French that Richard habitually spoke, but there seems no reason to doubt their authenticity.

This book is about Richard as a commander during the Third Crusade and concentrates on his military activities. However, no commander-in-chief of a multinational force can isolate himself and deal solely with military matters. Thus, there was an inevitable political dimension to many of his activities, and there were some periods when more of his time had to be devoted to resolving knotty political matters than to his military campaign. One aspect of this was that Richard could not avoid involvement in the question of who should be the ruler of the Kingdom of Jerusalem, nor could he set aside the difficulties of dealing with some very fractious allies, particularly the French and the ruler of the city of Tyre – Conrad, Count of Montferrat.

The Crusader Army

The Crusader army was divided into cavalry (i.e. the knights) and the infantry. The knights wore a suit of armour, carried a shield and their main weapon was the lance, although they also carried long swords and often some sort of mace. Discipline was fairly lax and the majority of the cavalry were inclined to be impetuous, preferring to charge rather than to devise a proper plan of attack. When they did charge, they tended to lack control and keep going, thus losing cohesion, scattering and laying themselves open to defeat in detail. The two groups that did have some discipline and a semblance of order were the military knights – the Templars and the Hospitallers – but they also showed a tendency to be very arrogant and sometimes seemed more interested in scoring off each other than in fighting Saracens. One of the main points of weakness for all Crusader knights was their horses, and the Saracens made deliberate efforts to hit them in the legs, thus forcing the knights to fight dismounted, where they were much more vulnerable.

The infantry wore thick leather jerkins, some reinforced with metal plates, while a few had chain-mail singlets underneath. The main purpose of this protection was to keep out arrows and it seems to have been successful since there are several Saracen reports of Crusader infantry continuing to march and fight despite ten or so arrows sticking out from their jerkins. All foot soldiers also carried packs containing their personal property and ten days' rations, which may have weighed as much as 70 lb. Such an outfit was extremely hot at the best of times, particularly so in a Mediterranean climate where infantrymen often suffered from severe heat exhaustion, it being by no means unknown for them to collapse and die on the spot. The infantry was divided into pikemen and archers, who carried crossbows (arbalests), and there was also a small number of engineers who were responsible for tasks such as mining, sapping, building and operating siege engines.

Finally, there was the baggage train, a large conglomeration of carts and their drivers, pack-horses, smiths, farriers, porters, laundrywomen, and the inevitable camp followers. This aspect of the Crusader army is discussed in more detail in Chapter 12.

The Royal standard was a vital tactical device, serving both to provide a rallying point and as a signal that while it flew, the battle still raged. It consisted of:

> A very tall pole, as it were the mast of a ship, made up of most solid timber, well jointed, cunningly carved, and covered with iron, so as not likely to fall a prey to sword, or axe, or fire. On the very top of this mast floated the royal flag – commonly called the *banner*.

This heavy device was mounted on wheels and drawn by horses, with a guard of specially chosen soldiers. The whole apparatus impressed the Saracens who commented that it was as high as one of their own minarets.

The Saracen Army

The Saracens had a much higher proportion of horsemen, who wore a lighter armour and rode faster horses than the Crusaders. Many carried bows, which they could use with great accuracy while on horseback, although their arrows were lighter than those used by the Crusaders and lacked penetrating power. Attacks were always accompanied by much noise from drums and musical instruments and troops shouting 'Allah akbar!' Two contemporary Crusader descriptions give the picture, the first describing the noise during a set-piece attack:

Moving ahead of the emirs [knights], there came a band of trumpeters and other men with drums and tabors; there were [men] who had no other labours, except upon their drums to hammer and hoot, and shriek and make great clamour.

The second concerns the Saracen cavalry harassing a Crusader column:

The Turks were not loaded with armour like our men, and with their ease of movement distressed us so much the more severely; for the most part they were lightly armed, carrying only a bow, or a mace bristling with sharp teeth, a scimitar, a light spear with an iron head, and a dagger suspended lightly. When put to flight by a stronger force, they fled away on horseback with the utmost rapidity ... If they see their pursuers it is their custom to turn back – like the fly which, if you drive it away, will go but when you cease it will return.

In general terms, the Saracen tactics were to harass the Crusaders whenever they were on the move, using pinprick attacks and constant fire from bowmen, trying all the time to cut off individuals or groups to be defeated in detail. The main Saracen force generally left the Crusaders alone in their campsites, but employed bedouin auxiliaries to infiltrate in order to kidnap or kill a few men and thus cause uneasiness and fear in the remainder.

Sources

The Third Crusade is among the first military campaigns for which contemporary accounts from both sides are available. I have taken as my primary source that attributed to Ambroise and generally referred to as *Itinerarium Peregrinorum et Gesta Regis Ricardi*, and all quotes in the text are from that book unless otherwise attributed. I have also referred in my research to *The Life of Saladin* by Kadi Bohâdin, and the works of Roger of Howden and Richard of Devizes.

There is some academic disagreement as to precisely who wrote the *Itinerarium Peregrinorum* but, whoever the author might have been, there can be little doubt that he actually took part in the scenes he describes, since his text has an immediacy and a *feel*, which shows that he was there. More than that, he adds many detailed touches which indicate to a soldier that the author knew what he was talking about. The description of the column being so densely concentrated that 'its members marched so close together that an apple could not be thrown to the ground without touching the men or their horses' has the ring of authenticity, as does: 'Our armour and breastplates became fouled with rust and could not be restored to their original brightness by any amount of rubbing'.

Perhaps more than this, however, are two descriptions of relatively minor incidents. The first occurred during Richard's operation at Jaffa (modern Tel Aviv) when the king and his companions made camp in the open and were very nearly taken by surprise by what would be described today as a 'snatch squad'. Fortunately, according to Ambroise:

> God, taking care lest the unbelieving should surprise His own champion while asleep, inclined the mind of a certain Genoese to go forth into the neighbouring plains at dawn. As he was returning he heard with astonishment the neighing of horses and the tramp of men, and saw the gleam of helmets against the distant sky.

Any field soldier will immediately recognise that the Genoese soldier who ventured a short distance from the campsite after a night's sleep, was answering the 'call of nature' rather than that of the Almighty, and it is clear that this is what the writer was referring to; indeed, it is probable that his contemporaries would have read it in this way.

The second is the following description:

> The horses and beasts of burden, affected by the cold and rain, were unable to proceed through the mud, but fell famished and knocked up beneath their loads. The drivers, in bitterness of spirit, raised their hands in anguish to heaven, and uttered imprecations approaching even to blasphemy.

Again, a modern soldier can picture the scene precisely – he has almost certainly seen the same thing many times during his service – as the frustrated drivers shake their fists at the sky and the air turns blue with their language. Indeed, it would appear that some aspects of a soldier's life have changed remarkably little over the past 900 years.

Names

The use of names in this book requires a brief word of explanation. The people who conducted the Crusades came from a wide variety of nations in central, northern and western Europe. They were sometimes referred to as Latins, because they followed the Roman Catholic rite, to distinguish them from the followers of the Greek Orthodox rite, who were called Greeks. In the Middle East, the local people referred to the Franks, a word which sometimes covered all people from western Europe, but was also used specifically to cover those Christians who had settled in the Middle East after the First and Second Crusade. In this book the term Crusaders is used, which simply describes the men and the undertaking they were involved in, and is what they themselves used.

Like the Crusaders, their opponents were an amalgam, which in this case included Arabs, Egyptians, Kurds, Syrians, Turks and other Middle Eastern ethnic groups, who were united by their common religious faith – Islam. This group too can be described in a variety of ways, the

Crusaders sometimes referring to them as Turks, Infidels, Mussulmen or Muslims. Here they are referred to throughout by the term most commonly used by the Crusaders themselves – Saracens – which was derived from the Greek expression *sarak nos* and simply means 'someone who comes from the east'.

The Crusaders generally referred to their destination as *Outremer* meaning 'beyond the sea', but once they had established themselves there, the territory was split into the Kingdom of Jerusalem and various principalities and counties. Here the designation Holy Land is used, since it was a territory of great religious significance to both Christianity and Islam. Within the Holy Land, most places have three names: the twelfth-century Arabic version, the contemporary name given by the Crusaders, and the modern name, which may be either Israeli, Palestinian or Turkish. As far as possible, this book employs the name used by the Crusaders.

The two great forces in the Third Crusade were led by King Philip and King Richard. King Richard's troops comprised men from the territories he ruled, which included England and Wales, Normandy, Poitou and Aquitaine. Once in the Holy Land, a number of other contingents joined Richard's service, either because their leader was somehow related or owed allegiance to him, or because he paid them. Richard was generally described as the King of England so for simplicity, and to avoid awkward terminology, all these groups are collectively referred to as the English forces. By the same token, Philip's followers comprised the men from his kingdom of France, the force led by the Duke of Burgundy and a number of foreign contingents, such as that from Genoa. These are collectively referred to as the French forces.

CHAPTER 1

The Background to the Third Crusade

The conduct and performance of King Richard I of England as com-mander-in-chief in the Holy Land, his achievements and failures whilst there, and the many problems he faced, can only be understood in terms of the historical context in which he found himself. The greatest aim for many of the Christians of western Europe in medieval times was to visit the Holy City of Jerusalem before they died – by the eleventh century there was already a long tradition of pilgrimage, which was by no means confined to the wealthy aristocracy. For a long time there were no major obstacles to pilgrimage, but in the middle of the eleventh century the Christians of western Europe began to be alarmed by reports of the growing successes of the Seljuk Turks against the Fatimid caliphs of Cairo, the former's conquest of Syria and Palestine causing particular concern. More Turkish successes followed; they captured Jerusalem in 1071 and shortly afterwards defeated the Byzantine army at the Battle of Mazikert. What caused the greatest indignation, however, was that the Turks started to harass Christian pilgrims on their way to and from Jerusalem.

The First Crusade

The formal and public origin of the First Crusade can be identified exactly, as the undertaking was proposed by Pope Urban II in a sermon made at Clermont Ferrand, France, on the afternoon of 27 November 1095. This was greeted with such enthusiasm that the Pope instructed his bishops to broadcast the news, which was welcomed throughout western Europe, with people immediately starting to volunteer in large numbers. The Pope's plan was remarkably well thought out, requiring national groups to assemble and to start their march to the Holy Land in August 1096. Each group had to be self-financing (thus avoiding any charges on the Church) and the various contingents would make their own way to Constantinople, capital of Byzantium. Then, in cooperation with the Byzantine emperor and his army, they would expel the Turks from Anatolia and drive forwards, through Syria and into Palestine, eventually reaching the Holy City, which they would restore to Christian control. What would then happen was left, perhaps deliberately, somewhat vague, although it must have been clear that the Crusaders would not be able to just walk away and allow the *status quo ante* to be restored.

Three large groups assembled as planned in August 1096 and made their separate ways to Constantinople. First to arrive was a group led by Godfrey of Bouillon, Duke of Lower Lorraine, which was composed of people from his own duchy, including his brother, Baldwin of Boulogne, plus numbers from Germany and northern France. This group made remarkable progress, following the Rhine southwards and then continuing to the Danube, which they followed through Hungary and Serbia and into Bulgaria; they then turned south once again and crossed the mountains, reaching Constantinople on 23 December 1096.

The second major group was led by Duke Hugh de Vermandois (the

King of France's brother), Duke Robert of Normandy and Count Stephen of Blois, and was composed of a mixture of Frenchmen, Normans and Englishmen. They crossed the Alps and marched down the length of Italy, where they spent the winter, although Duke Hugh went ahead and, despite being shipwrecked, managed to reach Constantinople in early December 1096. The remainder waited until spring and then sailed from the ports of Apulia on the Italian coast to Dyracchium (now Durazzo in Albania), from whence they followed an old Roman road, reaching Constantinople in May 1097, the last of the groups to arrive.

The third group assembled in southern France, under the leadership of Count Raymond of Toulouse and the Bishop of Puy. These men marched eastwards, and, having brushed aside some resistance to their progress in the Alps, they carried on down through Slavonia to the Adriatic. They then followed the Dalmatian coast until they reached a point where they could strike east towards Constantinople, arriving in late April 1097.

There was also a fourth group, which had not been in the original plan. This consisted of Normans from southern Italy, led by Duke Bohemond of Taranto and Count Tancred, who had been inspired by contact with Crusaders from the other groups passing through their territory en route to the Holy Land. Thus, although the last to start, they were actually the second to reach Constantinople, arriving on 26 April 1097.

It is not surprising that the Byzantine emperor, Alexius I Comnenus, and his people found the sudden arrival of these multitudes of foreigners very threatening; the interlopers came in huge numbers and there were frequent misunderstandings and many examples of bad behaviour. The emperor also wanted to ensure that the considerable military potential of the Crusaders should be employed to his advantage, so he pressed the leaders of the four main groups into agreeing that they would hand over to him any former Byzantine territory that they captured. The Crusader leaders did not favour such a demand, but they eventually found themselves with no choice but to agree and they duly set off from Constantinople in May 1097. Their first objective was Nicaea, then the capital of the Anatolian Turks, but when they arrived the emperor persuaded the garrison to surrender to him rather than to the Crusaders. The Crusader army then advanced to Dorylaeum, where they soundly defeated the main Seljuk Turk army (1 July 1097) before crossing the Anatolian plateau, despite constant attacks from marauding Turks.

In September, and by prior agreement, the column split into two. Tancred and Baldwin of Boulogne broke off, with their followers, to take Tarsus. That achieved, this group then split again, with Tancred moving into Celicia, while Baldwin crossed the Euphrates in October and established himself as the first Count of Edessa, thus protecting the north-east flank of further Crusader advances. Meanwhile, the main body pressed on only to find themselves held up at Antioch, which held out much longer than expected, the siege lasting from October 1097 to June 1098. Then, as soon as the siege had been successfully concluded, the Crusader army was attacked by a Turkish relief expedition, which had been sent to try to save its comrades, but arrived just too late. The Turks, however, were defeated on 28 June 1098.

The Crusaders then paused for five months before starting the final leg of their long march, eventually moving slowly down the coast, carefully avoiding Saracen-held cities in order to conserve men and resources. They crossed into the Holy Land in May and arrived outside the walls of Jerusalem on 7 June 1099. The city was held by a strong and well-prepared Egyptian garrison, but the Crusaders were also strong and in excellent heart, since their goal was, quite literally, before their eyes. Just before the siege began they welcomed reinforcements from Genoa, who had reached the Holy Land by sea and brought much needed siege machines with them. The actual siege was surprisingly short and the Crusaders took the place by storm on 15 July, whereupon the gates were closed and every non-Crusader – man, woman and child – was massacred in the name of 'purifying' the Holy City.

Once this disgraceful episode had run its course, the leaders met and elected Godfrey of Bouillon, Duke of Lower Lorraine, as ruler of the newly won city and the surrounding territory – he was offered the title of king but modestly declined. Godfrey then led this particular Crusader army on its last campaign, defeating an advancing Egyptian force at Ascalon (12 August). Following this, the majority of the Crusaders, having fulfilled their vow to free the Holy City, left for home, leaving Godfrey and a relatively small garrison to control the conquered territories.

The First Crusade was a most remarkable undertaking, involving the assembly of disparate groups, long marches across Europe and then a combined fighting advance across Asia Minor and down to Jerusalem. Nothing like it had ever been attempted before; it involved close cooperation between many nationalities, most of whom had been in conflict with each other for centuries, and was achieved without any formal command structure. However, it also left a hostage to fortune, because there was now a European outpost in the Middle East that was self-governing and without any direct formal link or allegiance to any one nation in western Europe. Its overall loyalty was to the Pope, but the kingdom would inevitably have to call on western Europe for help – and, in particular, military assistance – if it was threatened by a resurgence of Islamic power.

The High Tide of Crusader Power in the East

In order to control their newly conquered territories, the leaders of the First Crusade established a number of new states. The first, the

Principality of Antioch, covered much of the south-eastern part of the Anatolian peninsula, extending along the Mediterranean coast from Tarsus to Jabala and with a considerable hinterland, some of which bordered on the second of these new Crusader fiefdoms, the County of Edessa. Crusader princes ruled Antioch until 1268, but Edessa, which lay well inland and had no natural borders, was the shortest lived of the Crusader states, being conquered by the Turks in 1150 and never regained by the Crusaders. The County of Tripoli lay to the south of the Principality of Antioch and did not come under full Crusader control until 1109 when the fortress of Tripoli fell after a five-year siege.

The Seigneurie of Oultrejourdain (which means 'beyond the Jordan') covered the Crusader territory east of the River Jordan, the first seigneur being appointed by the King of Jerusalem in 1115. He was duly succeeded by his son, but this man had to be removed by the king in 1132 and was replaced by one of the king's court officials, Pagan the Butler. The latter proved to be fully equal to his task, bringing his territory under firm control by means of a network of castles, one of which was Kerak of Moab, that dominated the main inland caravan routes from Egypt and Äilat, at the head of the Gulf of Aqaba, to Damascus. Taxes were imposed on the caravans and Kerak thus became a very fruitful source of revenue.

Jerusalem

Possession of Jerusalem and some sort of control over the person who ruled it were central to the whole Crusader undertaking. The first ruler, Godfrey of Bouillon, died in 1100 and was succeeded by his brother, Count Baldwin of Edessa, who had no reservations about accepting a royal title, becoming King Baldwin I. The throne thereafter became hereditary, although, as will be seen, there were several unique features, which caused frequent problems, not least to Richard when he took part in the Third Crusade. (See Appendix C for a table of the rulers of Jerusalem 1099–1192.)

The first of these peculiarities was that while the King of Jerusalem was named as such, and was anointed and treated as a monarch by his people, western Europeans certainly did not consider him equal to existing monarchs, such as the kings of England or France. Indeed, they often regarded him as taking precedence according to any title he held in his native country; i.e. as a duke or count in France or Italy. The second peculiarity was that while the title was hereditary, it was also subject to confirmation by a council of barons. Thirdly, within the hereditary principle, the title passed on the death of an incumbent to his eldest surviving son, or, in the absence of a son, to the eldest surviving daughter, although it was her husband who then became king.

Reinforcements

The success of the First Crusade encouraged further support from western Europe and three separate groups followed the landward route, passing through Constantinople in 1101–2, but each was totally defeated during its crossing of Anatolia. Also, in the first decade of the twelfth century two Scandinavian groups reached the Holy Land. The first was led by Eric the Good, King of Denmark, travelling overland through Russia. The second was a Norwegian group led by the joint king, Sigurd Jorasalafar, who left home in 1107 and travelled entirely by ship, across the North Sea, down the Atlantic seaboard to Gibraltar and then through the Mediterranean to Acre, which was reached by the sixty-odd surviving ships in 1110. Sigurd visited Jerusalem and took part in some fighting before returning to Norway. It was an epic undertaking, although by no means the first time that Viking longships had operated in the Mediterranean.

The Second Crusade 1147–9

The relatively easy early Crusader victories were due in large part to the lack of unity among the scattered Saracen powers and although they continued to resist the Crusaders, they had no real success until the rise to power of Imad ed-Din Zengi. Known in the West as Zanggi, his first major victory came with the taking of the city of Edessa in 1144. This caused alarm in western Europe and the Pope proclaimed the Second Crusade in 1145, with the participants setting forth May–June 1147, although this time the leaders of the main contingents were emperors and kings rather than dukes and counts. Thus, the Holy Roman Emperor, Conrad III, and the German contingent left Nürnberg in May 1147, while King Louis VII left France a month later. During the First Crusade a number of leaders and knights had been accompanied by their wives, and this was repeated on the Second Crusade, with Louis being accompanied by his queen, the redoubtable Eleanor of Aquitaine. She took with her a train of 300 ladies, who, on suitable occasions, wore specially designed suits of armour, although, as far as is known, they never took part in any fighting.

On leaving Constantinople, Conrad marched his army (which was actually more of an ill-disciplined mob) straight across Anatolia, where they ran out of food and water. The army was massacred at Dorylaeum (25 October 1147), Conrad himself being one of the very few survivors. Louis was some distance behind Conrad, but followed the coastal road around the Anatolian peninsula until reaching Attalia, where he transferred his court and most of the cavalry to ships, sailing direct to Antioch. The elements of the cavalry left behind in Attalia objected strongly to being abandoned in this fashion and chartered their own ships, leaving the infantry and walking pilgrims to continue as best they could by land. With no cavalry protection and constantly harassed by

Saracens, this party lost well over half its number on the way to Antioch. After a brief stay in Antioch, Louis and his court sailed on, arriving in the Holy Land in May 1148 and going straight to Jerusalem where, at long last, they joined up with Conrad, who had arrived, less his army, a month earlier. Louis, Conrad and King Baldwin III of Jerusalem then attacked Damascus, which their combined forces reached in July, but the expedition was an absolute disaster, and following heavy losses they returned to Jerusalem. Once there, the three leaders quarrelled so seriously that Conrad and Louis took what remained of their armies and left for home.

The new Saracen leader, Nur al-Din, continued his conquests, culminating in the capture of Egypt in 1169, during which his forces were led by a little-known general, Saladin. Nur al-Din died in 1174, the undisputed ruler of a territory stretching along the Mediterranean coast from what is now Libya in the West, through Egypt, to the borders of Palestine. He also ruled much of the Levant and as far east as the Tigris Valley, leaving the Crusader territories surrounded on three sides.

The great Saracen leader, whose correct name was Salah ad-Din Yusuf, but which was shortened by the Crusaders to Saladin, was a Kurd, born in what is today Iraq in 1138. He joined Nur al-Din's army in 1152 and his exceptional abilities ensured such rapid progress that in 1169, aged just thirty-one, he was appointed commander of the army and vizier of Egypt. Following Nur al-Din's death in 1174, Saladin consolidated his position, taking Damascus in 1174, Aleppo in 1183 and Mosul in 1186, although he always looked upon Egypt as his powerbase, and the source of most of his manpower, supplies and riches.

Once he had stabilised his own Islamic territories, Saladin felt ready to undertake what he had always known would be his ultimate task – the expulsion of the alien Crusaders from Palestine. His invasion of the Kingdom of Jerusalem began in May 1187 and the then king, Guy, immediately mobilised his forces. The two armies met at a place called the Horns of Hattin in Galilee, on the east side of the Lake of Tiberias, where the Crusaders were utterly defeated. King Guy and most of the leaders were captured, together with the revered fragment of the Holy Cross, which up till then had always accompanied the Crusaders into battle. Saladin then swept through the country in a lightning campaign, taking one stronghold after another, climaxing with Jerusalem on 4 July. This left Tyre as the last major Crusader region standing out against him.

News of these disasters had a devastating impact upon western Europe with Pope Gregory VIII announcing the Third Crusade on 29 October 1187. So intense was the feeling that the three greatest European monarchs of the new generation – Friedrich I Barbarossa, the Holy Roman Emperor, Philip II of France and Henry II of England – all 'took the Cross', although it was two years before a start was made, by which time Richard I had succeeded his father as King of England and ruler of large territories in western France.

The Crusader Position in the Holy Land

That the Crusaders ruled the Holy Land tends to conceal the fact that their total numbers were actually very small and their indigenous army was correspondingly weak, unless reinforced from outside. The cavalry was formed exclusively from knights and the superior ranks of the aristocracy, and in the early 1180s (i.e. before the Battle of Hattin) the Kingdom of Jerusalem could field 700 knights. To these could be added contingents from the autonomous County of Tripoli and Principality of Antioch, which had military establishments of 200 and 700 knights, respectively. However, they would never have sent all of these and left their own defences bare, probably only sending a total of about 300 between them. Added to this were the knights of the military orders – the

Hospitallers and Templars – which normally fielded about 300 each, with possibly rather more Templars than Hospitallers. There were also some 300–400 clergy in the Holy Land, a large proportion of whom served as knights when the need arose, with bishops often in command. Finally, there were usually a small number of knights and their entourages either passing through the Holy Land on a pilgrimage or on short stays. Thus, at the most, the cavalry force would comprise about 1,700 men, and rather less when manning defensive garrisons, sickness and wounds were taken into account.

There was also an infantry force, the bulk of which was provided by the descendants of sergeants who had come out with the First and Second Crusades and then settled. Some of these were known as 'turcopoles', people who had one European parent and the other from the local population, usually from one of the Christian communities. Mercenaries were also present both from western Europe and the Middle East, who simply rented out their services to the highest bidder. The army of the Kingdom of Jerusalem could probably count on some 7,000–8,000 infantry, of which about 6,000 came from the kingdom itself, 1,000 from Tripoli and Antioch and 1,000 from the military orders.

Over the years following the success of the First Crusade the great majority of the Christian settlers adopted local habits and customs to varying degrees. It was only common sense to adopt local dress as this was far more attuned to the great heat than that of western Europe, while local houses were also well-adapted to the climate. Mixing with Muslims also exposed Christians to Islamic culture and some at least learned to speak and write Arabic. The settlers also adopted some of the weapons of the Muslim armies and used lighter types of armour, better suited to the climate than the patterns they had brought with them from northern and western Europe.

All this did not mean that the gulf between Christian and Muslim had been bridged, but it did give visiting Crusaders the impression that the people they were supporting had relaxed their standards. When the members of the Third Crusade arrived they professed to be shocked at the extent to which the settlers had adopted local ways: they were therefore labelled as degenerate and enfeebled, both as soldiers and Christians. Traces of this attitude have been perpetuated down the centuries, although there seems little to justify it either on the battlefield or off it, and there were as many ineffective soldiers among the newly arrived Crusaders as among those descended from the settlers. Indeed, as will be seen, in an era when maps were almost totally unknown and the few that did exist were extremely inaccurate, and when there were few, if any, books describing topography and climate, these local Crusaders were absolutely essential sources of information to the visitors.

The military orders were not a financial drain on the kingdom as they quickly accumulated enormous funds and became self-sufficient. In peace they policed the pilgrim routes, provided medical care and hospitals for the pilgrims, and built huge and very strong castles at no expense to the king, while in war they provided well-disciplined and self-sufficient bodies of well-armed men. On the other hand, their only earthly allegiance was to the Pope (who was far away), their loyalty was to their order rather than to the kingdom, and as they became richer and more powerful they behaved with increasing arrogance and wilfulness. The problem was exacerbated by the fact that the two principal orders, the Templars and the Hospitallers, developed an intense rivalry, which more than once resulted in serious problems.

Events Prior to Hattin

The events in the Kingdom of Jerusalem leading up to the Third Crusade were more than usually complicated and had a heavy influence on events throughout Richard's time in the Holy Land. King Amalric died in 1174 and was succeeded by his son, Baldwin IV, who was not only just thirteen years old but was also suffering from leprosy. The government was administered for several months by the seneschal, but he proved unpopular and was replaced after a few months by Count Raymond of Tripoli, a close relative of the boy-king, who was appointed regent. There now followed a period of even more intense court intrigue than usual, as various elements within the court sought to use their networks of family relationships to jockey for power. They divided broadly into two parties. One, which might be termed the 'easterners', was led by Count Raymond of Tripoli and was mainly composed of those descended from the original settlers in the Holy Land: their main aim was to remain in control of the kingdom, but coexist with their Arab neighbours. The other party, the 'westerners', was mainly composed of more recent arrivals under the leadership of Count Reynald of Châtillon: they wanted confrontation rather than accommodation with their neighbours. Matters were exacerbated by the fact that the military knights also split into two, with the 'eastern' party supported by the Hospitallers and the 'western' party supported by the Templars.

The new king, Baldwin IV, was initially successful and managed to hold his own in a series of battles with Saladin in the years 1176–9 until a two-year truce was signed in May 1180. But the whole situation was complicated by the fact that the boy-king could never have children, making it necessary that the next-in-line, his sister Princess Sibylla, be married, so that her husband could become king and one of their children succeed to the throne in due course. The man selected, William of Montferrat, was an Italian and considerably older than his bride, but nevertheless a sound choice, and he married Sibylla a few days after his arrival in the Holy Land in October 1176. Unfortunately, he died of malaria in June 1177, although a son (also called Baldwin) was born a few weeks later. However, the problem of the future kingship immediately resurfaced, since it was clear that Baldwin IV would not survive until his infant nephew came of age. Thus, after yet further scheming, a young French noble, Guy of Lusignan, was selected as Sibylla's second husband and he was duly summoned from France. As soon as he arrived it became clear that he was a foolish and erratic young man, but it appeared that there was no alternative, so the marriage went ahead, causing endless complications over the next decade, not least for Richard.

Throughout the history of the Kingdom of Jerusalem there was never a situation so bad that one of its nobles could not make it worse. In this case it was Reynald of Châtillon, Seigneur of Oultrejourdain, who broke the two-year truce with the Saracens by attacking one of their caravans passing through his territory. Reynald knew perfectly well that each side had guaranteed the other's merchants freedom of passage, but he was both exceptionally arrogant and very greedy, and simply ignored any effects his rashness might have. Saladin was furious and complained bitterly to Baldwin IV, demanding compensation, and although the king had no hesitation in agreeing the justice of the Saracen case, Reynald refused to back down. Then, by mischance, some 1,500 Christian pilgrims landed in error in Egypt and were immediately arrested and held hostage by Saladin pending return of the stolen property, but even then Reynald refused to comply.

As a result, Saladin led a punitive expedition from Egypt, following a circular route which took him deep into the desert so that he approached the kingdom from the north-east, totally outflanking Baldwin's army which was waiting for him further south. Baldwin, who was still leading his army in person despite the advanced state of his leprosy, rushed north and the two armies met below the Crusader castle of Belvoir in a long and hard-fought battle which was, effectively, a draw. However, the strain was too much for the king who was taken ill, and while still on his sickbed was persuaded to appoint his sister Sibylla's husband, Guy of Lusignan, regent.

While Saladin was involved in Galilee in mid 1182, Reynald of Châtillon decided to undertake a raid southwards, taking with him some prefabricated galleys. Having captured Äilat at the head of the Gulf of Aqaba, these galleys then raided deep into Muslim territory. Reynald's men caused a lot of damage and took a great deal of booty, but they were eventually defeated by an Egyptian fleet under Admiral Husam. Most of Reynald's men were captured and executed, but he managed to escape and Saladin, swearing that he would exact revenge, invaded Palestine in September 1183. Guy mobilised all available Crusaders to resist him, but Saladin encircled the Crusader army at the Pools of Goliath. There then followed a lengthy and inconclusive stand-off, which was only broken when the Saracen forces withdrew across the Jordan. The short campaign had revealed Guy to be weak, indecisive and cowardly; so bad, indeed, that King Baldwin IV deprived him of his post as regent, took back the reins of government, and declared that his nephew Baldwin (his sister Sibylla's child by her first marriage, who was now six years old) was to be his heir.

Saladin twice attacked Count Reynald's stronghold at Kerak, but on both occasions the strength of the huge fortress, coupled with the imminent arrival of a relieving army from Jerusalem prevented him from achieving his objective and he conducted prudent withdrawals. Then in March 1185, King Baldwin IV died in Jerusalem. He was one of history's most tragic characters, being intelligent, extremely courageous and possessed of greater vision than his courtiers, but also saddled with leprosy, a disease which literally ate him away, and surrounded by particularly quarrelsome and factious courtiers. He was succeeded by the seven-year-old Baldwin V, with Count Raymond of Tripoli as his regent, but the boy reigned for only a short time, dying in August 1186 and causing yet another major crisis. His mother, the Princess Sibylla, was the only genuine claimant to the throne, but an important group of nobles still had grave reservations about her husband, Guy of Lusignan, and tried hard to prevent her accession. However, Sibylla's faction, with strong support from Reynald of Châtillon, managed to win control of Jerusalem and she was duly crowned queen, following which she crowned Guy king.

The confusion was made yet worse when the objectors to Guy nominated Humphrey of Toron and his wife, Princess Isabella, as the rightful king and queen. However, Humphrey, an even weaker character than Guy, slipped away to Jerusalem and there voluntarily did homage to Guy, after which the latter's position was secure. Even so, some continued to object; Prince Raymond III of Antioch refused to swear allegiance to the new king, as did Raymond of Tripoli, who retired to his castle at Tiberias. Saladin, whose intelligence concerning events in the various Crusader communities was always excellent, sought to stir things up and released some of Raymond of Tripoli's knights he was holding prisoner.

Matters continued in this way for several more months until December 1186, when, despite knowing that another truce was in force, and with almost unbelievable disregard for anyone's interests other than his own, Reynald of Châtillon attacked yet another Saracen caravan, killing the Egyptian escort, making the travellers hostage and taking all the loot back to his castle at Kerak. Once again Saladin protested, but King Guy proved too weak to take any action against his unruly vassal and it is scarcely surprising that Saladin saw this as a reason for war. Several of the great barons opposed to Guy hastened to sign truces with Saladin, whereupon Guy marched against one of them, Raymond of Tripoli, to bring him back into line. There then followed another series of misunderstandings and miscalculations to which the Kingdom of

Jerusalem seemed so prone, which resulted in the Saracens killing some ninety Templars and Hospitallers (including the latter's Grand Master), whereupon Raymond repudiated his truce with Saladin and made allegiance to Guy.

This led directly into the brief and, for the Crusaders, disastrous Hattin campaign, already described, following which some 300 Hospitallers and Templars were executed at Saladin's orders. This was precisely the same fate that the military orders regularly meted out to captured Saracens, although somewhat surprisingly, Saladin did not execute the Grand Master of the Temple. The great Saracen general also spared King Guy, thus unintentionally opening the way for the next stage in the war between his people and the Crusaders.

Thus, the setting for the Third Crusade was that western European Christians had established a new kingdom at the far end of the Mediterranean, which had run its own affairs for some ninety years. But, as Saladin had so ably demonstrated, the situation was fundamentally insecure, since the number of Crusaders resident in Outremer was always relatively small, they were a long distance from western Europe if help was required, and, to cap it all, the nobility wasted great amounts of energy on interminable and complicated quarrels. Nevertheless, Jerusalem remained the most potent symbol for the Christians of the West and Saladin's rapid conquest, culminating in the disaster at Hattin, called for revenge. But worse was to come.

CHAPTER 2

The Start of the Third Crusade

The ever increasing threat from the Saracens had been identified well before the disaster at Hattin, and regular pleas were sent to western Europe for military assistance. The most immediate result was a regular flow of small parties of knights and their retainers, who would stay to fight for a year or two, visit Jerusalem and then return home. This was, however, by no means sufficient and anybody who gave the matter serious consideration realised that if the Christian hold on the Holy Land was to be maintained then what was needed was another full-scale Crusade, despite the disasters of the Second Crusade. A further factor, separate from the religious aspects, was the numerous links between those who had settled in the Holy Land and their families in western Europe – many of the nobles in Outremer were of French origin, while Henry II of England was the head of the House of Anjou and a cousin of King Baldwin IV of Jerusalem.

By 1185 the threat to the Holy Land was so serious that Baldwin IV sent a very high-level mission to western Europe, consisting of the Patriarch of Jerusalem and the Grand Masters of both the Hospitallers and the Templars, although even such illustrious figures could stir up no more than a tepid response. The situation was suddenly and completely changed, however, by the news in 1187 of the disastrous defeat at Hattin, and when this was followed by the fall of Jerusalem, it was realised that the situation was desperate, possibly even fatal. Many men immediately took the vow, although, as often happened throughout the Crusading period, by no means all those who did so had any serious intention of actually going on Crusade.

Two of those who took the vow were King Henry II of England and King Philip II of France, but the situation between their two countries was such that neither could afford to go on a Crusade if the other did not. As a result, they met on 21 January 1188 and agreed to renounce their own quarrels in order to go Crusading together. Henry, however, was old, tired and ill, while Philip was too interested in regaining his own lost territories in his native France, so a Crusade did not happen. Henry's son and heir, Richard, also took the vow at about this time, with the difference being that he had every intention of Crusading, as he soon proved. This was undoubtedly due, at least in part, to his Christian beliefs, but the possibility of military glory and his mother's reminiscences of how she had gone to Jerusalem as Queen of France, may also have had something to do with it.

Preparations

Henry II died in July 1189 and Richard's enthusiasm to undertake a Crusade became his highest priority, although he had three major concerns to resolve before he could leave his kingdom. The first was to raise the large amount of money he knew would be needed and the other two were the potential predators who might seek to steal part, perhaps even all, of his kingdom while he was away: Philip of

France from the outside and his own brother John from the inside.

Richard was crowned in Westminster Abbey on 3 September 1189 and immediately turned his immense energies to preparations for a Crusade. The measures he employed were so thorough and implemented so rapidly that it is clear that he must have given careful thought to the subject over a period of many months. As a result, his agents chartered and assembled ships, and procured warlike stores and supplies, while Richard himself took measures to ensure the governance of the kingdom during his absence.

One of Richard's top priorities was to raise money, without which nothing could be achieved. He realised that he had to: buy or lease many items prior to departure; carry with him sufficient funds to pay his troops and mercenaries; pay for logistic support, such as transport, food and fodder; charter shipping; and have some money left over for unforseen contingencies. He proved particularly adept and imaginative at this. One method was to make those who had taken the Crusader's vow and now wished to withdraw pay compensation. Another was summarily to deprive many officials of their posts and then offer them the opportunity to buy them back. Richard also made a deal with the King of Scotland, under which a number of outstanding disputes were settled, so that the security of England's northern border was assured during his absence, but even the Scottish king could not avoid contributing – the Scottish exchequer paid 10,000 marks into the Crusader fund. It was said at the time that 'the king put up to sale everything that he had', and even Richard himself said that he would sell London if only he could find a buyer.

Richard held a series of meetings with Philip, who, although eight years younger had been king for ten years: one was on 29 December 1189, another on 20 June 1190 and yet another at Vézelay in the first week of July 1190. Among the many agreements reached, it was decided that all spoils would be shared equally, and that their armies would assemble at Messina at the invitation of King William II of Sicily, who was married to Richard's younger sister, Joanna, where whoever arrived first would wait for the other.

The Journey to Sicily

Richard and Philip then set out, arriving at Lyons in mid July 1190 where they crossed the Rhône, suffering their first mishap when the bridge gave way. Surprisingly, only two men drowned, but much inconvenience was caused until Richard personally designed and supervised the construction of a floating bridge, made of boats lashed together.[1]

From Lyons they separated, with Philip and the French making their way overland to Genoa, while Richard and his army headed south, arriving at Marseilles on 31 July, where the English king expected to find his fleet waiting for him, but it had not arrived. Some English Crusaders, headed by the Archbishop of Canterbury, then hired galleys to take them direct to the Holy Land, which they reached on 16 September 1190. Richard, however, had other plans and having waited a week he hired two large busses[2] and twenty well-armed galleys, sailing on 7 August. He arrived at Genoa on 13 August to discover that Philip was already there, but sick. Philip asked for the loan of five galleys, but when Richard offered only three Philip turned them all down.

Richard then made his way down the coast of Italy, sometimes aboard ship but also covering considerable stretches overland on horseback. From 28 August to 8 September he was in the Naples area and then rode to Salerno where on his arrival he learned that his fleet had already arrived at Messina. So, he ordered the fleet to put back to sea to collect him, thus enabling him to make a splendid arrival, as befitted his status, on 23 September 1190.

Unfortunately, King William of Sicily had died the previous

November, and since there were no children from his marriage to Joanna the legal heir was Constance, who was married to Heinrich Hohenstaufen, the eldest son of Friedrich Barbarossa. In order to prevent the Sicilian throne passing to a German, however, the Pope had given the throne to Tancred, an illegitimate cousin of William's.

Sicily

Thus, the Crusaders arrived to find a somewhat uneasy political situation, which was made worse for Richard because Tancred was refusing to give Joanna the money and property due to her under her husband's will. In fact, the relationship between Richard's followers and the locals was bad from the very start, with the Sicilians making the English Crusaders feel most unwelcome, refusing even to allow them to buy food. Matters quickly deteriorated to the point where Richard felt it necessary to seize two castles on the Italian mainland, so that he could install his sister Joanna in one, and his important stores and supplies in the other.

Then on 4 October, a fight between Richard's men and the citizens of Messina got so out of hand that Richard stormed the city and took it over. His men looted the place until they were stopped by the king, at which point Philip, who had done absolutely nothing to assist his fellow Crusaders, demanded that his flag should also be placed on the battlements and that he should have half the booty. Indeed, Philip became so difficult that Richard threatened to pack up and proceed on his own, at which point Philip backed down.

The Sicilian ruler, Tancred, had initially favoured Philip, but he now saw that Richard was the more powerful and determined of the two, and came to terms with him. This was formalised in a treaty which included the betrothal of Richard's nephew, Prince Arthur of Normandy, then aged four, to one of Tancred's daughters. With matters thus temporarily resolved, Richard ordered that the booty be returned to the townsfolk, a decision not entirely popular among his own men who used such loot to help defray their costs. As soon as he learnt of this, however, Richard distributed gifts (presumably of money) which satisfied all, while Tancred presented Richard with four large transport ships and fifteen galleys.

In late February 1191, Richard broke off his long-standing engagement to Aloysia, Philip's sister, who had been resident at the English court for some years in anticipation of her marriage. One of the reasons given for terminating the engagement was that she had previously been seduced by King Henry II, her future father-in-law. Whether this was true or not, Philip did not stand in Richard's way and yet another treaty was signed between Philip and Richard on 25 March, following which Philip and the French left for the Holy Land.

The final major event of Richard's stay in Sicily was the arrival of his mother, Queen Eleanor, who had gone to northern Spain to collect Richard's new fiancée, Princess Berengaria, and then brought her to Reggio to meet her son, a remarkable journey for a sixty-year-old lady in medieval times, but Eleanor was no ordinary woman. Richard went to Reggio to meet them both and escorted them to Messina where Eleanor stayed just four days before setting out on the return journey to England. Meanwhile, Richard and his men, their preparations now complete, set sail on the final leg of their journey to the Holy Land on 10 April 1191.

CHAPTER 3

The Cyprus Campaign

The next episode in Richard's Crusade seems to have been totally un-planned since it took place in Cyprus, an island he had never intended to visit, let alone conquer. The island is shaped like a saucepan, with a main body some 47 miles from north to south and 100 miles from east to west, with a 'pan handle' – the Karpas peninsula – sticking out to the north-east, which is 43 miles long but with an average width of only 6 miles. The island, the third largest in the Mediterranean, has an area of 3,600 square miles and is approximately the same area as East Anglia in the United Kingdom and about two-thirds that of Connecticut in the United States.

The main geographical features are two mountain ranges, with the Kyrenia range in the north running parallel to the northern edge of the island and extending into the Karpas peninsula. This range is extremely rocky and unbroken, its highest point being some 3,350 feet above sea-level. The second range, the Troodos Mountains, covers most of the south-western portion of the island and is more broken, its highest peak being Mount Olympus, some 6,560 feet . The remainder of the country, particularly that between the two mountain ranges, is a mixture of reasonably fertile farmland, especially in the west, but with areas of treeless, and generally waterless, scrub-covered plain.

Prior to Richard's arrival, sovereignty over the island had changed according to the rise and fall of the empires in the eastern Mediterranean. It was ruled by the Assyrians from the eighth century BC until 550 BC when the Egyptians took over, followed by the Persians in 525 BC and then a short period (333–323 BC) under Alexander the Great. With his death, Egypt once again took control, until losing it to Rome in 58 BC. Byzantium took over in 330 AD and ruled the island, more or less continuously, until 1183, when one of history's more bizarre figures appeared on the scene: Isaac Comnenus (1155–95), the grandnephew of Emperor Manuel I Comnenus (1143–80) of Byzantium.

As a young man Isaac was sent to Cilicia with the task of guarding the empire's eastern frontier, but he was captured by the Armenians who passed him to the Templars, whose stern religious beliefs did not prevent them from holding a fellow Christian for ransom. This was eventually paid by Emperor Andronicus Comnenus (1183–5) and shortly afterwards Isaac arrived in Cyprus where he produced forged imperial letters purporting to appoint him governor of the island. Once in firm control, Isaac proclaimed the island independent, with himself as emperor, and proceeded to impose a cruel and despotic rule, with murder, rape and plunder becoming the norm. The next Byzantine emperor, Isaac II Angelus (1185–95), sent a force to recapture the island, but Isaac Comnenus, aided by a Sicilian pirate, successfully repelled the mainland force and it was at this point that Richard became involved.

The Crusaders Arrive in Cyprus

Richard's fleet was large by any standard, numbering some 216 vessels of various types and sizes and, in accordance with the longstanding custom in the Mediterranean that winter months were unsuitable for sailing, he did not sail from Messina until 10 April 1191, just five days before Easter. This was likely to have been the very first prudent opportunity and a compromise between the requirements of the galleys and the sailing ships and, as events were to show, the fleet probably left too early. After only two days at sea, the winds increased, scattering the formation, but in the late afternoon the wind strengthened into a gale, which lasted through the night, causing great alarm, and many sailors as well as passengers were sea-sick. When it abated Richard gathered all the ships he could find – 'like a hen gathering her chickens' – until they reached anchorage off the island of Crete on 17 April. There, a systematic tally revealed that some twenty-five ships were missing, but after only a short stay Richard led the remainder on to Rhodes where he waited for ten days.

They sailed again on 1 May, and after a stormy and difficult passage through the Gulf of Satalia (modern Antalya), Richard's flagship had a chance meeting with a buss, which was returning to Europe from the Holy Land. The ship had sailed from Acre and the captain informed the king about the progress of the siege and that King Philip of France had already arrived and taken command. The captain also told Richard that Philip had erected several siege engines, but that some had been destroyed by the Saracens. Filled with renewed purpose, Richard and his fleet tried to make headway but were frustrated by another gale which blew them out to sea and they were, once again, scattered. Meanwhile, three of the missing ships had been driven towards Cyprus, which they reached on 24 April, but two were immediately forced ashore, with some of their crew and passengers being drowned, while the survivors were rounded up by the Cypriots and imprisoned in a fort. Stephen of Turnham, however, took his ship round to the southern coast and anchored off Limassol and on hearing that Crusaders ashore were under attack, he dispatched a landing party which rescued some of them. The self-styled emperor, Isaac Comnenus, was alarmed at the news of armed men landing on his island and rushed to Limassol, arriving on 2 May to find the foreign ship still at anchor. On being told that the passengers included the dowager Queen of Sicily (who was also the sister of the King of England) and a princess (who was about to become the King of England's wife), he realised their potential political and ransom value, and sent several invitations and gifts of food and wine to tempt them ashore. The two ladies, quite correctly fearing a trap, stayed aboard.

Richard, together with part of his fleet, arrived off Limassol on 6 May, where he was informed what had happened and immediately sent messengers ashore, demanding the release of the remaining prisoners and the goods the Cypriots had purloined. Isaac Comnenus responded that he was an emperor and thus superior to a mere king, such as Richard, and added some very offensive oaths to his message. His troops, grabbing anything they could lay their hands on, including old barrels, casks and doors, started to build barricades on the beach to prevent a landing.

Unfortunately for the 'emperor', he had chosen quite the wrong man to offend, and with a cry of 'To arms!', Richard and his men embarked in small rowing boats and set out for the shore. One group, led by Richard, headed straight for the beach, while a second group attacked five galleys moored in the harbour. The main group was held offshore for a time and the issue seemed to be in the balance, as both sides pelted each other with arrows, javelins and rocks. Realising that the impasse must quickly be broken or there would be a disaster, Richard leapt into the shallows and led the way ashore, where he became embroiled in hand-to-hand combat. Seeing this, his men stormed ashore after him and after a brief fight the Crusaders had established a firm beach-head.

Richard saw that a pause would be fatal and having driven the Cypriot army from the beach, he and his men harried them through the town and out the far side. Richard had found a lance in the city and espying Isaac Comnenus, shouted repeated challenges to single combat, but the 'emperor', very wisely, affected not to hear and kept going. Limassol was soon firmly under English control, so Richard had the two royal ladies brought ashore, while his Crusaders helped themselves to the riches of the city.

A Brief Campaign

Isaac Comnenus pitched camp five miles from Limassol, and thinking that Richard had no horses, announced his intention to his men to give battle the following morning. Richard, however, used the cover of darkness to get fifty horses ashore – a major achievement in its own right – and had them exercised to recover from their long voyage from Sicily. He and his knights left the town at 2 a.m. the following day and attacked one of Isaac's outposts at dawn, forcing the men to flee towards Isaac's camp in the next valley. Unfortunately, the Crusaders' pursuit was hampered by the unfitness of their horses, which could only move slowly, giving Isaac time to rally his men, who outnumbered Richard by a very considerable margin and so, for a moment, the Crusaders paused. Indeed, so heavily were the odds stacked against them that a clerk ventured to suggest to the king that it would be wise to defer attacking such a large and well-armed enemy. Richard gave a classic reply: 'Sir clerk, as for our professions, you had better employ yourself in writing and leave war to us ...'.

Richard sensed that the enemy leader was indecisive and that, despite their numbers, his troops were wavering, so he did what always came naturally to him in such circumstances: he lowered his lance, dug in his spurs and charged straight for them, followed by his knights. Such was the ferocity of his charge (and so little used were Isaac and his men to dealing with real soldiers) that Richard broke through the enemy line and laid into them with his sword. Discovering that these were not the recalcitrant peasants they normally had to face, the enemy quickly broke and were pursued by the Crusaders for two miles, during which Richard captured Isaac's personal banner. However, the Crusaders' horses were now too tired and Richard had to give up the chase; he and his knights returned to Isaac's camp to help themselves to the plentiful supply of booty.

On 11 May three galleys arrived from the Holy Land, carrying Guy of Lusignan, the King of Jerusalem, and his brother Geoffrey to ask for Richard's support. Their immediate problem, they told the King of England, was not so much the Saracens as King Philip, who, since his arrival in Acre on 20 April, had been trying to ease Guy off the throne and replace him with the ruler of Tyre, Marquess Conrad of Montferrat. Richard immediately promised his support and also gave the impecunious king generous presents including, according to Ambroise, 'two thousand marks of silver and twenty cups of the value of a hundred and five marks, of which two were of the purest gold'.

The following day, 12 May 1191, Richard and Berengaria were married in the chapel of St George, Limassol, following which Berengaria was crowned Queen of England.[3] It was a very grand occasion at which the king was 'cheerful to all and showed himself very jocose and affable'. The air of optimism was strengthened when more of the king's galleys arrived, and these, together with five galleys captured from the Cypriots, brought his fleet to forty armed galleys and sixty other ships, all of very good quality.

Despite having given the Cypriot forces such a battering, Richard did not overlook the possibility that they might counter-attack, and he insisted that his army should be ready at all times, with observers posted outside the city, and sentries at the gates and on the walls. At this juncture, the Hospitallers proposed a meeting between Richard and Isaac Comnenus, to which both agreed and the meeting was held on a plain outside Limassol. Richard, who clearly understood the necessity of impressing his opponent, arrived dressed in all his finery and mounted on a particularly splendid Spanish charger. After considerable discussion it was agreed that Isaac would swear fidelity to Richard, provide five hundred knights for the Crusade, hand over his castles, and pay 3,600 marks as reparations for Crusader losses. Following detailed scrutiny by legal experts the agreement was duly signed by the two rulers, Richard returning the imperial pavilion, which had been captured several days previously, to Isaac. All appeared to have been amicably resolved. That night, however, Isaac seems to have changed his mind, escaping on Flauvel, a horse renowned for its speed.

It is not surprising that Richard was highly indignant and formed his men into three groups: two seaborne, one on land. The seaborne groups were headed by Richard and Robert of Thornham respectively – they sailed round Cyprus in opposite directions, seeking Isaac, but also taking the opportunity to capture coastal towns, castles and ships. The landward group was initially led by King Guy of Jerusalem who marched to Famagusta where he met Richard, who had sailed round. The bird, however, had flown and Richard took command of the land forces for a march on the capital, Nicosia. He was about to set off when a second delegation from Acre arrived, this time sent by the King of France, who urged Richard to make haste to the Holy Land where all were anxiously awaiting his arrival. The two French emissaries took it upon themselves to rebuke Richard for wasting his time in Cyprus, persecuting Christians and delaying in the purpose for which they had all come to the Holy Land – killing infidels. Richard was furious and having told them so in no uncertain terms, he set out, brushing aside a rather lacklustre ambush before he and his army reached Nicosia, where they were greeted as liberators.

Thereupon, Isaac and his dwindling number of followers retired to four great castles in the north at Buffavento, Kantara, Kyrenia and St Hilarion, where they planned to hold out until Richard moved on to the Holy Land, at which point Isaac would emerge and reimpose his rule. Richard was about to set out to attack Isaac when, as was to happen several times in the following years, he fell ill in Nicosia, and King Guy was dispatched, in his place, to seek out Isaac. There then occurred one of those totally unpredictable events, which happen throughout history. Isaac Comnenus was a born liar, a confidence trickster – he had hijacked an entire country – and a cruel and despotic ruler, but his plan to await Richard's departure was brought to nothing when King Guy captured Kyrenia castle and with it Isaac's beloved only daughter. Isaac was distraught and to ensure her safety he immediately offered to surrender, his one condition being that he should not be put in irons. Richard agreed, but showed a grim sense of humour by having his smiths produce a set of chains made of silver – shackled in these, Isaac was dispatched to the Crusader fortress at Marqab in Syria.[4]

By 1 June 1191, all of Cyprus was in Richard's hands and he returned to Famagusta.[5] After making arrangements for the administration of the island, he sailed for the Holy Land on 5 June in a fast galley, with his army following aboard slower vessels. The Cyprus campaign had been a masterly operation during which Richard had captured a large island, about whose geography and people he can have known very little and whose mountainous hinterland was custom-made for a long drawn-out defence – and all this with an army numbering less than a thousand.

A Valuable Acquisition

This was Richard's only campaign in the Mediterranean where he was in sole command of his own troops, and he conducted the operation with lightning speed, taking just fifteen days from arrival to departure. He was bitterly criticised, at the time by Philip Augustus and by others later, for 'wasting time' by attacking Cyprus instead of making straight for Acre, and was accused of personal aggrandisement. But, in view of Isaac's proven duplicity and, in particular, his alliance with Saladin, taking the island eliminated the threat of a hostile base astride the Crusaders' supply lines. Indeed, Richard ensured that the Crusaders had a very valuable forward depot, noted for its agriculture and vineyards, all within one day's sail of the Syrian coast. Richard also obtained much treasure, which was used to finance the Crusade. Finally, Richard did not conquer Cyprus for territorial gain, as proven by his subsequent sale of the island, first to the Templars and later, when they returned it to him, to Guy of Lusignan.

CHAPTER 4

Siege of Acre: 1189–91

Richard arrived in Acre on 12 June 1191, fresh from his triumphs on land in Cyprus and having defeated a mighty Saracen dromon while passing Beirut (see pages 162–64). He joined the Crusader army which had been laying siege to the city since 28 August 1189 and in order to understand the position in which Richard now found himself, it is necessary to review what had happened during those twenty-one months.

Acre, which was actually known to the Crusaders as St Jeanne d'Acre and is today known as Akko, lies approximately 10 miles north of Caiaphas (modern Haifa) and 30 miles south of Tyre. By the time of the Third Crusade it had been under Crusader rule for a little over eighty years and was a thriving centre of trade and a valuable sea port with a population of some 6,000, who were crowded into a maze of narrow streets. There were many churches and properties belonging to the military orders, but its greatest importance lay in its harbour and flourishing markets.

The city was built on a low-lying promontory, with a man-made harbour on its southern side. It was entirely surrounded by walls, which on the landward side were some 100 feet high and with the added protection of a 90-foot deep ditch on the outside, which was designed to prevent tunnellers, siege engines or towers approaching too closely. The harbour had been created by building a mole, which extended from the eastern wall to a rock, on top of which was a defensive tower known as the Tower of the Flies[6] and the harbour entrance was further protected by a heavy chain.

Saladin's Run of Victories

Following his success at Hattin (4 July 1187), Saladin swept the Crusaders aside, taking most cities and fortresses, such as Tiberias, with comparative ease. A few held out, one very honourable example being Ascalon. The defeated King Guy was brought there by his captors to plead with the garrison to surrender, which he had been promised would secure his release, but his pleas were rejected with disdain. The garrison surrendered on 5 September, but resistance had been such that they were granted the full honours of war by the victorious Saracens. The same could not be said of Acre, which had very strong defences but fell to Saladin's men after a surprisingly brief, almost token, siege and despite its governor, Joscelyn III de Courtnay, being one of the few Crusader knights to have escaped the debacle at Hattin.

Once in control of Acre, Saladin appointed his best engineer, Bahā' al-Dīn Qarāqūsh, in command, with strict instructions to bring the defences up to the highest state of readiness. The Saracen army then continued its conquests until it attained the ultimate prize, Jerusalem, on 2 October 1187. The one city that resisted was Tyre, held with dogged determination by an Italian, Marquess Conrad of Montferrat.

King Guy had been taken prisoner at Hattin and was held until April 1189, when, having sworn on oath that he would never again take up arms against the Muslims, he was released. As soon as he was at liberty, however, he quickly found a Christian priest who was prepared to inform him that such an oath to an 'infidel' could not be considered binding to a Christian prince, thus immediately (and most conveniently) clearing the way for Guy to set about recovering his kingdom. His first step was to attempt to establish a temporary capital at Tyre, but he was prevented from even entering the city by Conrad of Montferrat and so laid siege to it.

One of the recurring problems during this period in the Holy Land was that reinforcements would suddenly appear with little or no warning – those already engaged in the Holy Land seldom knew whom to expect, while the newcomers had little idea of what they would find when they did arrive. Just after the siege began both Conrad and Guy were surprised when two contingents of Italian engineers arrived, one from Genoa and the other from Pisa. These newcomers were treated somewhat rudely by Conrad, so they threw in their lot with Guy. Perhaps encouraged by these reinforcements, and in one of the most extraordinary decisions in military history, Guy suddenly ended his siege of Tyre in August 1189 and took his poorly organised army, consisting of approximately 600 knights and 7,000 infantry, but with the notable addition of the Genoese and Pisans, southwards to lay siege to the great fortress of Acre. Perhaps he hoped for a lightning victory, as had been achieved by Saladin two years earlier, but, if so, he was to find that he had very seriously under-estimated the strength of the defences and the determination of its garrison.

The Siege Commences

Guy's army arrived at Acre on 28 August 1189 and set up camp at Toron, due east and some three-quarters some three-quarters of a mile outside the city walls. This was on a hill, with a river running past its foot, and was intended as a forward base for the blockade of the city, although it subsequently also became the hub of the defences against Saracen attacks from inland. Meanwhile, the Pisan contingent occupied a strip of shore just north of Acre, which they managed to retain throughout the siege, providing the essential link with the outside world, through which all Crusader reinforcements and supplies had to pass.

On 31 August, Guy made a quick attack in an attempt to surprise the defenders, but it failed and both sides prepared for a long siege. Fortunately for the Crusaders, groups of Danish, Flemish, French and Frisian knights and their supporters, who had been en route to the Holy Land for many months, arrived in September. As Guy's men started to fortify their camp, the siege of the Muslim stronghold proved to be an effective rallying cry for Christians. As a result, further reinforcements began to arrive from Europe and from elsewhere in the Holy Land.

Saladin was initially taken by surprise, partly because yet another Crusader had gone back on a solemn promise, but also because the prospect of such a small and ill-equipped army overcoming the well-fortified garrison at Acre seemed very remote. Nevertheless, he arrived in mid September with a Saracen army and set up an armed camp a short distance inland from the Crusaders, sandwiching Guy's army between his force and the city walls. In two hastily mounted operations, Saladin sent a supply column into the city and also drove the Crusaders off a small hill that they had taken in order to dominate the road northwards to Tyre.

The Battle of 4 October 1189

Guy knew that he would only be able to concentrate on the siege if he could resolve the problem of the threat from Saladin at his rear. His first attempt to achieve this was made in a battle on 4 October, during which the balance swung backwards and forwards several times in the course of a bitterly fought day. From the moment he arrived, Saladin knew that he would be attacked by the Crusaders but, even so, when it came they managed to take him completely by surprise, emerging from their camp just after dawn with the Templars in the van. King Guy was in the centre accompanied by four knights carrying a silk cushion bearing the symbol of the Gospel – a substitute for the relic of the True Cross, which, of course, had been lost to the Saracens at Hattin.

Gerard of Ridefort, commanding the Knights Templar, opened the proceedings with an attack on the Saracen right wing, which was commanded by Saladin's nephew, Taqi al-Din. Taqi decided to entrap the Crusaders by feigning flight, a ruse which he knew from experience would make the Crusaders pursue him – all he then needed to do was allow them to become overextended (as they always did) and order his men to turn and attack. It was an audacious plan, but unfortunately for the Saracens, Taqi neglected to inform his uncle, so that when the army commander saw his right wing in apparent flight he misunderstood the situation and immediately dispatched reinforcements from the centre. This precipitate reaction caused severe problems, since it seriously disrupted the Saracen centre without doing much to help the right wing. The situation was made worse by Saladin dashing around the battlefield, trying to be everywhere at once, as a result of which he failed to exercise a proper control over events and was unable to redeploy his forces effectively to meet the changing situation.

Seeing the confusion in the Saracen ranks, the Crusaders seized their opportunity and King Guy led a charge against the Muslim centre, which severely rattled the Saracen troops, who gave way, with a number fleeing in disorder. As usually happened with cavalry charges, however, the momentum of their successful charge carried the Crusader knights some distance before their commanders could bring them under control, turn them around and lead them back to the battle.

There then occurred a series of comparatively trivial and totally unpredictable events, which resulted in the advantage swinging rapidly and arbitrarily between the two sides. The first of these occurred when the servants in the Saracen camp saw Taqi's knights riding to the rear pursued by Crusaders – thinking (as did Saladin) that they actually were in flight the servants leapt to the conclusion that all was lost. Knowing from previous experience that they would receive scant mercy from the Crusaders, the camp servants panicked, grabbed what booty they could from their masters' tents, and set out eastwards as fast as they could go.

The returning Crusader knights came across the almost empty Saracen camp, and exactly as the servants had feared, killed the few remaining guards and servants. They then set about some serious looting, which was always a prime consideration, as they sought to defray the great personal expense of taking part in the Crusade. So involved did they become that, through some extraordinary oversight, none of them cut down Saladin's tent, which would have been taken as a signal that the entire Saracen army had been defeated and could well have led to a great Crusader victory.

Nevertheless, the Crusaders were clearly winning when the second of these trivial and unpredictable events occurred. While the Crusader knights were pillaging the Saracen camp one of the horses threw its rider, a German knight, and, as frightened horses tend to do, it galloped away, by chance in the direction of the Crusader lines, leaving its rider stranded. Seeing this mishap, some foot soldiers ran after the horse in an attempt to catch it and return it to its owner, but, other Crusaders, espying a riderless, galloping horse hotly pursued by shouting, running men, assumed them to be fleeing from an advancing enemy and, taking alarm, began to follow them in ever increasing numbers.

Meanwhile, Saladin had brought his own men under control, and seeing the Crusaders starting to withdraw towards their own lines he led a charge into their rear, turning a disorderly withdrawal into a rout, in which many hundreds of Crusaders were killed. Total victory was now within Saladin's grasp, but at this point he, too, became a victim of arbitrary events, and was surrounded by his own knights who were furious that their property had been looted by their own servants, who were now leaving the battlefield in large numbers. Accordingly, they forced Saladin to turn his attention from finishing off the Crusaders in order to dispatch a group of cavalry to catch the thieves and to bring them and their booty back to the camp.

By the end of this eventful day a large number of Crusaders and a lesser number of Saracens had been killed, but strategically the situation had not changed at all. The Muslim garrison inside the walls was still besieged, Saladin's army had not broken the siege, and Guy's Crusader army was still intact, remaining, as before, sandwiched between two groups of Saracens.

The Siege Continues

The situation eventually reached a stalemate. The Saracen garrison in Acre was on very short commons but managed to survive, mainly due to the occasional ship breaking through the Crusader blockade. The Crusaders had surrounded Acre on the landward side and were able to obtain supplies delivered by ship, but not by land. They were not, however, strong enough to carry the city by storm, nor could they defeat Saladin's forces, which threatened them from the landward side. As for Saladin, he had sufficient strength to contain the enemy but could not prevent their continuing attack on the city.

As was liably to happen in medieval sieges, matters now settled into something of a routine. The Crusaders completed a massive trench around the landward side of the fortress, which was designed to prevent forays by the garrison, while their ships sought to impose a naval blockade. They also built earth walls around their own camp in order to protect it from attacks from the rear by Saladin. The Crusaders carried out periodic assaults and the defenders beat drums and fired flares to alert Saladin's camp, which then attacked the Crusaders in their rear.

As a result of Saladin's army being outside their lines, the Crusaders were totally cut off by land, but since their right flank rested on the sea they were able to maintain communications with the outside world. They were able to receive both supplies and reinforcements, either direct from Europe or from their supply bases at Tyre and in Cyprus. The numbers of men and horses increased out of proportion to the food and fodder available – all of which now had to be brought in by sea – and the Crusaders began to suffer from hunger and disease. Saladin, however, was not without problems of his own, since his army was being depleted by men returning home and he was left with insufficient numbers to carry out a serious attack on the Crusader camp.

The siege continued throughout the winter of 1189–90 with the Crusaders concentrating on building three immense siege towers. Then in March 1190, Conrad of Montferrat, temporarily reconciled with King Guy, brought a relief convoy from Tyre and broke through the Saracen naval blockade to bring some much needed supplies. The Crusaders cleared three approaches for the engines, and at the end of April the siege towers were moved until they were close up against the walls. All three towers were 100 feet high, so that the archers on the top floor were able to fire downwards into the city, thereby causing much mayhem among the defenders. The Saracens tried desperately to destroy the towers using Greek fire but failed, making a tentative offer to surrender, which was refused by the Crusaders. At this, a renewed attack was made on the siege towers led by an engineer who devised a new form of fire attack, as a result of which one tower was destroyed in flames, killing all those inside. On seeing this, the occupants of the other towers fled in panic and the Saracens sortied from the nearest gates to destroy these structures as well.

In May 1190 Saladin, having received some reinforcements, carried out a series of attacks on the Crusaders over an eight-day period, but by this time the latter had improved the defences of their camp with ditches and walls, and they managed to survive. Then, in late July, it was the Crusaders' turn to attack Saladin, but they too were repulsed with heavy casualties.

A few days after this attack, on 27 July, the Crusaders received unexpected reinforcements in the shape of a large French contingent under the command of Count Henry of Champagne. Henry was the nephew of both the kings of England and France and thus, despite the apparent disparity in their titles, he was considered senior to King Guy of Jerusalem and assumed command of the Crusader force.

Meanwhile, the Crusaders had turned their attention to a battering ram, which was constructed throughout the summer using the mainmast of one of the many ships stuck on the beach. It had a roof and was covered in animal skins that had been soaked in vinegar, supposedly to make the device fire resistant. However, when the ram was put into use in October, the defenders managed to destroy it with fire, as they had the towers earlier.

The Crusaders did not limit their attacks to the land and in September two very imaginative naval assaults were carried out. In one, a siege tower was constructed on a platform resting upon two galleys lashed together by ropes. It was then used to attack the Tower of Flies, which stood at the end of the southern mole, but, again, the defenders managed to set fire to the siege tower and it was destroyed. Next, the Crusaders tried to use fire themselves by sending a fireship into Acre harbour, but, although there were many Saracen ships in the harbour, little damage was done. Nevertheless, this was a remarkable operation and was one of the first – if not *the* first – recorded uses of such a tactic, which was to become quite common right through to the nineteenth century.

As the siege continued, conditions within the Crusader camp deteriorated rapidly. Hygiene was very poor and the campsite was filthy in the extreme, resulting in a great deal of sickness, mainly dysentery, and a variety of diseases including typhus and scurvy; indeed, over the entire period of the siege, far more Crusaders died from sickness than in military action. Nor was disease any respecter of rank. Both Queen Sibylla, the wife of King Guy, and her two daughters died on 1 October 1190 and later both King Philip of France and Richard of England were taken ill, the former losing his hair and nails (possibly caused by scurvy). To add to the Crusaders' problems there was rampant inflation and food was both very scarce and extremely expensive.

On 4 October, the survivors of the German Crusade arrived, but since their emperor, Friedrich Barbarossa, had drowned in Anatolia, they were now under the command of his son, Friedrich von Schwaben, a much less effective leader. However, they did bring with them a siege engine and a very large battering ram. A few days later, the advance guard of the English Crusaders arrived, led by Baldwin, Archbishop of Canterbury. It is also reported that another type of reinforcement arrived in October, in the shape of 300 ladies of 'easy virtue', who offered physical, rather than spiritual, solace to the weary Crusaders.

Meanwhile, the siege operations continued. The newly arrived Germans carried out an unsuccessful assault in November and by mid December the Saracen garrison inside Acre was on the verge of starvation and began another round of negotiations for a surrender. Once again, Saladin managed to stave off defeat by sending a large force of twenty-five ships, which fought their way through the Crusader blockade and averted the crisis inside the fortress.

The winter of 1190–91 was both bleak and very wet, and the unusually heavy rains so undermined the walls of the fortress that a part fell down, taking both defenders and besiegers by surprise. But then, when the Crusaders managed to organise themselves and attempted to carry out an assault, they were so hampered by the continuing rain that they failed – after a struggle, the Saracens managed to repair the breach. By now, all involved were suffering intensely, although Saladin managed to get another convoy into Acre during February, while the Crusaders were saved by a convoy which arrived in March. The sickness in the Crusader camp continued, claiming Friedrich von Schwaben in January, leaving the German contingent leaderless until Duke Leopold of Austria arrived in April.

King Philip II and the French force arrived at Acre on 20 April 1191, where they immediately threw themselves into the battle, but Richard and the main body of the English, as described in the previous chapter, were delayed by storms and the brief Cyprus campaign, finally arriving on the beach beside the Crusader camp on 12 June 1191 to great acclaim.

Once Richard came ashore the Crusaders' command situation changed yet again. One faction under Philip consisted of the French and the Genoese, the other of Richard, supported by King Guy and the Pisan contingent. Richard, however, was in a much better financial position and was able to attract many uncommitted knights to his banner by offering them more pay than King Philip of France. Neither king was more powerful than, nor would they give way to, the other, so there was a period where the two were in an informal command-sharing arrangement. This did not stop either of them from trying to gain an advantage over the other, and Richard's more powerful personality tended to outshine that of the weaker Philip.

Richard startled everyone by offering to meet Saladin face-to-face – while refusing to attend in person on the grounds that commanders did not meet until the terms had been agreed, he did send his brother Saphadin. The two men spent three days in discussions without reaching any significant agreement, although they achieved a degree of mutual respect that was to endure throughout the conflict.

Richard then suffered from his first bout of the local sickness, and while he was 'hors de combat', Philip led an attack on Acre, which, for a variety of reasons, turned out to be an expensive failure. Firstly, many of Philip's soldiers, particularly the mercenaries, including, critically, the engineers, had transferred their loyalties to Richard and did not take part in the attack. Secondly, Saladin carried out a diversionary raid on the eastern end of the Crusader trenches, which enabled the garrison inside Acre first to repulse Philip's attack and then to venture outside the walls to destroy many of the French siege engines.

Richard immediately demonstrated a special aptitude for siege warfare. He had a great interest in siege engines, often taking the opportunity to aim and fire them in person, and also designed mangonels and even a portable wooden fortress nicknamed 'Mategriffon' (literally, 'death to the greeks', i.e. infidels) which was built at Messina while he was there and then brought, via Cyprus, to the Holy Land. The great majority of these siege engines were built and operated by the different national contingents, but one was paid for by donations from individual Crusaders and operated by an international crew. It was known as 'God's Own Catapult', and perhaps because of this auspicious name, was successful in shattering one of Acre's strongest walls. Thus, throughout this period the siege engines continued battering, while sappers were digging away at the walls. Several targets were under attack, but Richard's main concern was the Maledicta tower, which was under almost continuous bombardment.

Richard also devised a system of employing his men in alternating infantry assaults and engineering work, which, by ringing the changes, kept them fresh. Determined to bring matters to a successful conclusion, Richard also had an increasing number of siege towers brought into action and moved them all close to the walls from where archers could make life very difficult for the defenders.

The Final Stages

Matters were now moving inexorably towards a climax – on 2 July 1191, a section of the wall near the Maledicta tower collapsed and the following day the French assaulted the breach but were driven back. On the same day, the Saracen general, Taqi, tried to lead a relief force into Acre but was beaten back. Then, on the night of 5 July, continued mining under the Maledicta tower resulted in a further collapse and a furious battle quickly developed as the Crusaders sought to consolidate their gains by getting rid of the debris (which was in the way of an assault), with Richard offering huge sums to soldiers to carry it away. Despite heavy losses this was partially achieved and the French put in a second assault on 7 July, followed on 11 July by Richard with a force made up of English and Pisans.

All of these assaults were repulsed due to the difficulties of getting through the rubble, so Saladin, realising that the fortress's days were numbered, attacked the Crusaders from outside, but was beaten off. With that the Saracen garrison realised that nothing more would be achieved by holding out. So, on 12 July, the city commander offered terms, his first proposal offering to give up Acre 'free and clear', return the fragment of the Holy Cross to the Crusaders together with 200

Christian captives held in the city, and hand over fifty of his own men as hostages.

As was normal in such negotiations, this first offer was rejected out of hand by the Crusaders, so the Saracens came up with a second proposal, which, in addition to surrendering the city and returning the fragment of the Holy Cross, included the return of 2,000 noble Christians and the handing over of 500 Saracen prisoners. The Saracen garrison would abandon the city, each man taking just his clothing, with all weapons, food and other property to be left in Acre (where it would, of course, become loot for the victors). The Saracens also offered money to be given personally to King Richard and King Philip and a further, but lesser, amount to Conrad of Montferrat who had negotiated the surrender (but none, it should be noted, for King Guy). Finally, some valuable Saracen nobles would be given as hostages against good faith. A significant feature of this offer was that the great majority of the returned Christian prisoners, the money and, of major importance to the Crusaders, the fragment of the Cross, would have to come from outside the city, but Saladin was not consulted as to whether he could meet such terms. Despite this, the terms were agreed and the hostages were duly delivered to the Crusaders on Friday 12 July 1191, with the settlement of the balance due to take place on 12 August.

Before the Saracens emerged from the battered city, heralds went throughout the Crusader army proclaiming that there was to be no molestation, injury or insult to the captives. These men, women and children were then put into a guarded camp on the plain, but a day or two later were taken back into the city and housed in accommodation which had been found for them.

It was the custom when a city fell for the various victorious leaders to place their banners on the ramparts, particularly of a tower or wall which they themselves or their men had taken, and at some point very soon after the occupation of Acre, Richard was riding through the streets when he spotted a banner on a tower whose blazon he did not recognise. On asking, he was told that it belonged to Duke Leopold of Austria, to which he took immediate and great exception. Richard lost his temper, something most members of his family were prone to do from time to time, and had the banner ripped down and brought to him, whereupon it was trodden into the mud by members of his entourage. To cap it all, when he met the duke, Richard addressed him in a highly insulting manner, to which, of course, Leopold was unable to reply since Richard was a king. Why Richard should have taken such great umbrage has never been explained, but, whatever the reason, Leopold regarded the affair as a mortal insult and was able to take devastating revenge when he kidnapped Richard during his return journey to England.

The Massacre

The long siege so rashly initiated by King Guy twenty-three months earlier, ended in a Crusader triumph. However, any description of the fall of Acre would be incomplete without mention of the tragic sequel, which occurred on 20 August 1191, when the Crusader army gathered outside the walls of Acre and massacred virtually all the Saracen prisoners who had been captured when the city capitulated. This event has besmirched Richard's reputation ever since, and while some of the details of the events leading up to the massacre are disputed, the general outline is not.

The agreement concerning the capitulation of Acre was made between the Crusader commanders and the commanders of the Saracen garrison in the city, and Saladin was neither a party to the negotiations nor a signatory of the final document. Nevertheless, he never sought to dissociate himself from what had been agreed nor did he seek to evade obligations that had been placed upon him, except only in the matter of time. The deal was made on 12 July 1191 and the garrison commanders agreed that they would capitulate immediately and members of the garrison would be kept as hostages until the completion of three conditions: the fragment of the Holy Cross, captured by Saladin at Hattin, would be returned to the Crusaders; 1,600 Crusader prisoners held by Saladin would be released; and a large sum of money would be handed over, with 200,000 bezants being paid to each of the kings of England and France, and 14,000 to Conrad of Montferrat, who had negotiated the deal. It was also agreed that the delivery of the Holy Cross, the prisoners and the money would take place one calendar month from the date of the capitulation (i.e. 12 August); if these conditions were complied with the Saracen prisoners would be released, and if the conditions were not met, the prisoners would become slaves.

The Saracen hostages were split equally between the two kings and although Philip placed some of his share in the custody of the Duke of Burgundy, he took the most important of them with him to Tyre, where he handed them over to Conrad and then sailed for home. Richard, of course, needed these men to hand over to Saladin as his part of the agreement and he sent a message to Conrad on 5 August to return them forthwith, which Conrad refused to do, so Richard had to dispatch the Duke of Burgundy, who succeeded, returning with the prisoners on 12 August.

Meanwhile, there were repeated meetings between representatives of the two sides and Saladin appears to have done his best to meet his obligations. Just before the deadline, however, he informed Richard's emissaries that he needed more time, saying that he would immediately release such prisoners as had arrived and hand over the money then to hand. According to the customs of the time, this meant that the Crusaders would have remained in possession of some 3,000 Saracen prisoners until Saladin could meet the terms in full, but it was agreed instead to extend the deadline to 20 August, it being tacitly understood, again by the custom of the day, that the exchange would take place at midday.

Richard was desperate to move for a variety of reasons. Firstly, following the lengthy privations of the siege most of the troops were living a life of debauchery in Acre, and morale and the efficiency of the army were decreasing by the day. Secondly, the longer he remained inactive, the more time he gave Saladin to make preparations to counter the Crusaders' next move. And, thirdly, with Philip's return to France he needed to get home to defend his lands against the possible depredations of the French king, who, for very good reason, he did not trust. The greatest obstacle to all this was the large number of prisoners he held – if he took them with him they would form a huge, reluctant, ill-disciplined and discontented mass, which would slow down his advance, require a large guard force to prevent them from either escaping or being freed by the Saracens, and require food and water. But, if Richard left them in Acre, he would have to leave a large force behind to guard them, which he could not afford to do, while simply to release them would have been counter to every custom of the day and would have infuriated his own troops.

On 14 August, Richard moved most of his troops out of the city and set up his own tent on the plain in sight of the Saracen encampment. On 15 August, Saladin sent another message, saying that he was still having difficulties in meeting his obligations, and requesting a meeting with Richard on the following day. Richard awaited his opponent's arrival but Saladin did not come, and when the day of the deadline arrived Richard was still awaiting some response. None came.

The time for Saladin to fulfil his obligations was midday and once it had passed a council of the chiefs was called, where it was agreed that it was useless to wait any longer and that the hostages should be killed.

Accordingly, the Crusader army assembled on the plain and the hostages were led out, bound with ropes, and killed with spears and swords. As always, different figures are given, but it is generally agreed that well over 2,000, and possibly as many as 3,000 prisoners were massacred.

Richard never made any effort to evade the responsibility for what took place. Although the action was approved by the council of chiefs, he was the undisputed commander-in-chief at the time and on the spot throughout the day, and could thus have stopped the action had he chosen to do so. Some authorities report that the Duke of Burgundy and the French contingent undertook the massacre of King Philip's share of the hostages, and it is also clear that there were few, if any, dissenting voices either in the council or among the Crusader army as a whole.

Repellent as the massacre is to modern eyes, it is important that it should be judged in the light of twelfth-century morals and customs, and not by those of the twenty-first century. In those times, massacres were by no means uncommon: Saladin had ordered the execution of every Templar captured at the Battle of Hattin, a total of some 300. In the 1370s, the famous and greatly admired French knight, du Guesclin, captured large numbers of English prisoners on two separate occasions; some 500 on the first, considerably more on the second. Bitter wrangling broke out within his own ranks as to whom each prisoner belonged and therefore who would gain the ransoms, so the French commander ended the quarrels by killing the lot.[7]

A further factor is that the end of a siege was considered in a unique light. A besieged garrison was usually given an early opportunity to surrender and, if the offer was accepted, would almost invariably be granted generous terms. If, however, the garrison decided to fight to the finish, this would involve the attackers in many very costly attempts to carry the walls; as a result, once the defenders capitulated, the victorious soldiers considered that they had the right to loot and pillage, and the longer and bloodier the siege had been, the more savage they were. When the Crusaders captured Jerusalem on 15 July 1099, for example, the soldiery murdered virtually every inhabitant, probably numbering about 40,000 men, women and children. Despite the lengthy privations experienced by the Crusader army before Acre, the end of the siege had been very civilised and the soldiery had been denied what many of them would have regarded 'their right'.

Contemporary writers describe the massacre, but even the Arab Bahā' al-Dīn does not dwell over long on it and there is no evidence that the Saracens bore the Crusaders any long-term ill will. Bahā' al-Dīn's comment is probably the most apt:

> The motives of this massacre are differently told. According to some, the captives were killed by way of reprisal for the death of those Christians who the Mussulmans had slain. Others again say that the king of England, on deciding to attempt the conquest of Ascalon, thought it unwise to leave so many prisoners in the town after his departure. God alone knows what the real reason was.

CHAPTER 5

The March from Acre to Jaffa and the Battle of Arsuf

Having taken Acre, Richard had to decide on the Crusaders' next move. This was to be not only his first mobile operation since arriving in the Holy Land but also the first time he would be in sole and total command – commander-in-chief, in modern terms – since Philip Augustus had left for France on 31 July 1191. Although the French and some Germans were unhappy with the English king's assumption of this responsibility, there could be no real dispute since Richard was the only European monarch on the scene (the King of Jerusalem was very low down in the order of precedence), he was also paying almost everybody in the Crusader force and, finally, he was incontestably the most redoubtable fighter in the army.

For all the Crusaders there was no question that the ultimate destination was Jerusalem, but that was held by the Saracens and they would be unlikely to give it up easily. The problems facing Richard were:

❖ To move his complete army with sufficient people, equipment, siege train and supplies necessary for the siege of Jerusalem, which would undoubtedly be lengthy and difficult.

❖ To keep Saladin and his army at bay during the approach march.

❖ To establish a major supply base on the coast and then to keep the main supply route between that base and field army open, particularly during the siege.

❖ His multinational force was the only Crusader field army – if it was defeated there would be virtually no territory left and the Holy Land would be lost. He had, therefore, to maintain its integrity.

❖ His army was multinational, poorly trained and ill-disciplined, and had no collective experience of mobile warfare, having been bogged down for many months in the totally static siege of Acre.

These considerations left Richard with two main choices. First, he could head inland and pick up the North–South route which ran roughly from Nazareth, past Mount Tabor and then southwards past the Pools of Jacob and Ramla (Ramallah) to Jerusalem. He could reach this route via a number of cross-paths running roughly south-east from Acre–Nazareth, Caiaphas–Jenin, and Caesarea–Pools of Jacob. Such an advance would also threaten the main Saracen caravan route from Egypt to Damascus, which followed the Jordan valley. However, this would involve a long march – 130–150 miles, depending on the route – through difficult country. Also, the Crusaders' huge baggage train would, of necessity, have to follow valley routes, leaving the hills to the Saracens, which would give the enemy a major tactical advantage. In addition, the horse-carts, pack-horses and human porters of the baggage train would slow the rate of advance to a crawl, while the main supply route would be extremely vulnerable to Saracen attack, a problem that would increase with the distance from Acre.

The second choice was to march down the coast to Jaffa, a distance of some 80 miles, then strike inland to Jerusalem. This had a number of significant advantages, the first being that Richard would keep his strategic options open since, apart from turning inland towards Jerusalem, he could also keep going down the coast, thus threatening Ascalon, Darum and eventually Egypt – the political and financial heart of Saladin's empire. As well as this, by marching along the coast he kept his right flank totally protected by the sea, and most of the supplies and the siege equipment, plus any wounded, could be carried aboard ships, thus dramatically reducing the size of the supply column. In addition, the ships gave links not only to Acre, but also to Cyprus and western Europe.

It is impossible to ascertain the precise numbers involved,[8] but in the army that left Acre following the coastal route, Richard had under direct command his own Angevins, Normans and English. There were also a number of groups and individuals in his pay, including the Pisans, some Germans (the remnants of Barbarossa's expedition), a group of Hungarians under the Count of Hungary, and local Franks led by King Guy. Among the most militarily effective were the members of the military orders, of which the two principal groups were the Templars and the Hospitallers, each led by their Grand Masters. Last but by no means least, there was the French contingent led by the Duke of Burgundy, whose relationship with Richard was, at best, strained, since the duke queried almost every strategic decision Richard made and, on occasions, even withdrew altogether.

Despite the support from the sea, there was also a supply train of carts and porters. Women were specifically forbidden from taking part in the march, although washerwomen were allowed, on the grounds that they were deemed not to present 'an occasion for sin'.

For his part, Saladin had the only Muslim field army, with which he had regained most of the Holy Land. But, were he to lose to Richard, the

Crusaders would once more recapture Jerusalem forcing him, if he survived, to start his reconquest all over again. Therefore, he could be reasonably certain that Richard must, sooner or later, head for Jerusalem, although the Saracen leader had always to be aware of the possibility that the Crusaders might make a diversion to Egypt. Once Richard set out on his march southwards along the coast, Saladin could rule out each route towards Jerusalem as the Crusaders passed it, but he could never be quite certain of Richard's ultimate destination. So, he sent his men ahead to burn crops and to destroy castles at Caesarea, Arsuf and Jaffa before the Crusaders reached them. The main threat he posed to the Crusaders was that as their column moved slowly southwards his army kept pace with them, just out of range on their left flank, skirmishing daily, snatching any foragers who ventured too far outside the Crusader lines and infiltrating their camps by night.

Marching

The Crusader's formation on each day's march followed a more or less standard pattern, with minor alterations to suit the day's requirements or changes in the terrain. The most important consideration was that the Crusaders had command of the sea and, with the exception of Days 13 to 16, the right flank rested securely on the shore. The knights formed the main body, moving in between three and five dense groups, normally riding stirrup-to-stirrup and with their horses nose-to-tail. At the head of the column was the advance guard and at the tail a rearguard, both considered to be positions of such great importance and prestige that they were invariably provided by the Hospitallers and Templars, who usually rotated the two duties on a daily basis.

The infantry had two tasks. First, there was a dense column on the left (landward) flank of the column of knights, whose primary task was to prevent the Saracens getting close enough to attack the knights' horses. On the seaward side of the column of knights was the baggage train, composed of horse-drawn carts, pack-animals and porters, and which also included those 'camp followers' permitted to accompany the troops. Many of the porters were found from the infantry and alternated with those forming the screen, thus sharing the burden and the danger.

Few accurate timings for the start and completion of each march are available, so the speed of advance cannot be decided with any degree of precision. However, the pace would have had to take into account the width, length and density of the column, the mixture of horses, men and wheeled carts, the difficulties of command-and-control, the heat, the poor state of the track, the activities of the Saracens and the complications inherent in the movement of any large body of people. Thus, the maximum rate of advance could have been not more than 2 mph and was more probably 1 mph or less, although the column did manage to cover 13 miles on Day 9.

The conditions for the Crusaders were appalling. The days were blisteringly hot, with temperatures in late August reaching 27° C, sometimes rising to 38–40° C. The effects of such high temperatures were complicated by the Crusaders' warm clothing, armour and chain-mail, the horses defecating, and the fact that very few, if any, of the Crusaders washed, the military knights on principle and the others because they knew no better. The going was hard as the only routes were tracks, most of them Roman roads which had not been maintained for centuries, and which were in many places overgrown with dense bushes and scrub. Inevitably, the head of the column quickly destroyed what little coherence there was in the track, leaving those behind to struggle as best they might through loose sand or dense mud.

Richard was, however, as considerate of his troops as the circumstances allowed. He tried to reduce the effect of the heat by making early starts – at 3 a.m. on 1 September, for example – marching only in the mornings and seldom for more than one day at a time, interspersed with rest days. The proceedings were as well organised as possible in contemporary circumstances, with harbingers (harbourers) going forward in an advance party to reconnoitre and mark out the next night's campsite, there was at least some discipline in the campsites, and a reasonably assured resupply from the ships.

South of Merla (i.e. Day 10 onwards) the conditions became so bad that soldiers often fainted from the heat. A lucky few were transferred to a ship to be taken to the next halting place; some, however, collapsed and died on the spot and were simply left. In the campsites, the Crusaders were attacked by tarantulas, which gave a very painful sting to the unwary, although the soldiers persuaded themselves that these could be repelled by noise, so there was a constant cacophony through the night.

The March from Acre to Jaffa, August–September 1191

Day 1: Thursday 22 August

The army set out from Acre on Thursday 22 August and despite minor attacks from the Saracens, they crossed the River Belus (Nahr el Namein), which enters the sea a short distance south of Acre, and set up camp on the coastal plain. On this first day, they progressed barely 2 miles but were moving deliberately slowly to give everyone the chance to get used to the formations and command system. This was necessary not only because the army had spent the past two years in static siege warfare, but also because the past weeks had been devoted to debauchery in Acre, so there was a need to give everyone time to settle into a new routine.

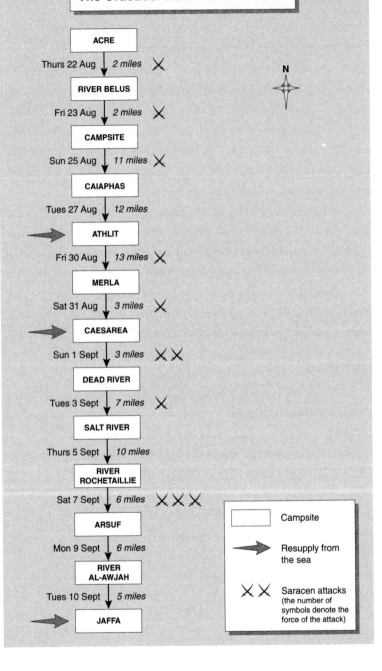

The Crusader march Acre to Jaffa

ACRE

Thurs 22 Aug — 2 miles ✕

N

RIVER BELUS

Fri 23 Aug — 2 miles ✕

CAMPSITE

Sun 25 Aug — 11 miles ✕

CAIAPHAS

Tues 27 Aug — 12 miles

➡ ATHLIT

Fri 30 Aug — 13 miles ✕

MERLA

Sat 31 Aug — 3 miles ✕

➡ CAESAREA

Sun 1 Sept — 3 miles ✕ ✕

DEAD RIVER

Tues 3 Sept — 7 miles ✕

SALT RIVER

Thurs 5 Sept — 10 miles

RIVER ROCHETAILLIE

Sat 7 Sept — 6 miles ✕ ✕ ✕

ARSUF

Mon 9 Sept — 6 miles

RIVER AL-AWJAH

Tues 10 Sept — 5 miles

➡ JAFFA

	Campsite
➡	Resupply from the sea
✕ ✕	Saracen attacks (the number of symbols denote the force of the attack)

Days 2–3: Friday 23 – Saturday 24 August

The second day's march was also short, with the column making its way along the narrow plain between the River Belus on its left and the sea on its right. This constriction forced the column to extend and the rear part of the baggage train became vulnerable, at which point the Saracens charged in, breaking through the infantry cordon and getting in among the wagons, even pushing some of the Crusaders onto the beach. A messenger was promptly dispatched to inform Richard, who, with a group of knights, came galloping back and drove off the attackers. Having covered 2 miles during the day the army made camp on the coastal plain, on a pleasant site which included some wells and cisterns.

The day's adventures provided a valuable lesson for Richard, who saw the need for even stronger advance and rearguards, while the Crusaders as a whole learnt the value of cohesion and obedience to orders. Richard was determined not to overstretch his men as they settled into the marching routine, so they remained in the same site for the whole of the third day and night.

Days 4–5: Sunday 25 – Monday 26 August

The army made an early start on the fourth day, undertaking the first long march of the operation – a distance of some 11 miles – but with a definite goal to encourage the marchers, Caiaphas. Again, they spent two nights on the site and the men took the opportunity to sort out their equipment and loads, throwing away a lot of gear which had seemed so essential just five days earlier, before they left Acre.

The Saracens also started a process of shadowing the Crusader army, keeping the bulk of the army poised for a major attack should the opportunity offer itself. Light cavalry kept a very close watch and darted in to kill or snatch small groups or individuals; any live prisoners were taken to Saladin, who, with the memory of the killing of the garrison of Acre fresh in his mind, questioned them and then invariably ordered them to be killed. Saladin also regularly carried out personal reconnaissances of the path ahead of the Crusaders, examining their route and possible campsites with a view to attacking them. His headquarters and the baggage train moved 5 to 10 miles inland, parallel with the coast.

Days 6–8: Tuesday 27 – Thursday 29 August

Early on the morning of the sixth day the column left Caiaphas, heading west on the old Roman road which took them around the foot of Mount Carmel and then south. The Templars were in the van and the Hospitallers in the rear, but on this occasion at least, the Crusaders' left flank was well-protected by the steepness of the hill, which prevented the Saracen cavalry from attacking them. The route itself, however, was overgrown, which caused particular problems for the men on foot as the bushes and shrubs tore at their skin and clothing. By about midday they were passing the town of Capernaum, which had been flattened by Saracens, and they stopped for a brief rest and something to eat. They then pushed on, arriving at that day's goal, 'Casal of the Narrow Ways' (later named Athlit), in the late afternoon. The campsite was large and pleasant and the army remained there for three nights and two days. On the second day the sea train made its first appearance, bringing supplies and a few reinforcements.

Day 9: Friday 30 August

Refreshed by rest and heartened by the resupply from the ships, the army set out early on the morning of the ninth day on what was its single longest day's march – 13 miles to Merla. As usual, they were harassed by Saracen attacks and Richard once again led a charge to clear the route and, as so frequently happened, was very nearly captured.

Day 10: Saturday 31 August

Despite the exertions of the previous day, the Crusaders set out early on the morning of Day 10, heading for Caesarea, which, like all other towns on this stretch of coast, had been demolished by Saladin's men. By this time the heat was even more intense and the cover particularly sparse, so that men were dropping dead in the line of march and were buried, if at all, where they fell. Others, who were taken ill but had some prospect of recovery, were transferred to ships and taken on to the next halting place.

That afternoon the Crusaders pitched camp close to the River of Crocodiles (Nah'r Zerka) which reached the sea some 3 miles north of the partially destroyed town. As the campsite was being established, ships arrived from Acre bringing not only supplies but also large numbers of reinforcements, known to the marchers as the 'lazy folk', who had been reluctant to leave Acre and who had only now been prised away from the drinking dens and brothels.

Days 11–12: Sunday 1 – Monday 2 September

The following morning the army started off at about 3 a.m. and the open nature of the country gave the Saracens better than usual opportunities to harass the vast, slow-moving column. According to Bahā' al-Dīn, the Saracen drummers and trumpeters played, accompanied by incessant shouts from the Muslim troops of 'God is great' and 'There is no god but God', all the while firing arrows and making charges at the Crusaders, but the latter 'kept steadfastly in perfect formation, undismayed and undisturbed'. They occasionally scored some local successes, as, for example, in one skirmish in which a renowned Saracen warrior named Aisas Estoy (Ayaz the Tall) was killed. The column eventually arrived at a suitable river at about midday, although, since the watercourse was almost completely invisible under a dense matting of reeds and rushes, the Crusaders convinced themselves (almost certainly erroneously) that it had been deliberately concealed by the enemy as a trap. The Crusaders named the stream the Dead River (Flum Mort), but despite the inauspicious name, they spent two nights there.

Days 13–14: Tuesday 3 – Wednesday 4 September

It was already daylight when the army started off on Day 13, but the leading elements soon found that the route was so overgrown that progress was impossible, and they were forced to strike inland until they reached a road running parallel to the coast. Here, they were subjected to heavy attacks which forced them into an even closer array than usual but, despite such precautions, the Templars and a group led by the Count of St Pol lost so many horses that they were in despair. Once again, Richard was personally involved in beating off the attacks and was slightly wounded in one of the skirmishes. They camped that night at Salt River, but even with the resupply by sea on 29 August, food was becoming scarce and the majority of the men were now very hungry. As a result, one source of meat – horses which had died of wounds – had become desperately expensive. Richard stepped in once more, promising a live horse from his own stock to any knight who gave his dead horse to the soldiery. On the afternoon of 4 September Richard sent emissaries to Saladin proposing discussions.

Days 15–16: Thursday 5 – Friday 6 September

The column started its march at 3 a.m. on Day 15, while Richard went to the prearranged rendezvous to meet Saladin's brother, Saphadin, with Humphrey of Toron serving as interpreter, but no progress was made and the meeting broke up quickly. For most of the day the column, still on the inland track, marched through the Forest of Arsuf, the men being somewhat anxious due to a rumour that the Saracens intended to set light to the forest and burn them all. In the event, nothing happened, but when they emerged into the open they found the Saracen army drawn up for battle. The Crusaders set up camp on the north bank of the River Rochetaillie, 9 miles south of Salt River, and spent the next day in the same place, preparing for the major battle which they knew was to come. Thus, as so often in English military history – for example, on the nights before Agincourt (24/25 October 1415) and Waterloo (17/18 June 1815) – the two armies spent the night within sight of each other's fires, knowing there would be a battle on the morrow.

The Battle of Arsuf, Day 17: Saturday 7 September
The ancient site of Apollonia-Arsuf, by tradition the place where St George slew the dragon, is a plateau, bordered by a sandstone cliff over-looking a natural harbour (the site of the present-day town of Herzliya), about 9 miles north of Jaffa. The area had come under Crusader control in 1101, since when it had been the capital of a Frankish seigneurie, which had had a small castle built overlooking the sea. The Saracens had recaptured the town the previous year and had demolished the castle in the days prior to Richard's arrival. There is no doubt that Saladin delib-erately selected this site for the major battle he had been seeking since the Crusader march from Acre began.

Richard's plan for 7 September was to break camp at sunrise and to reach the town of Arsuf by midday, but since his men all knew that a battle was inevitable, they made even more careful preparations than usual. Once all was ready, the Crusaders crossed the River Rochetaillie and then, with the right flank again resting on the sea, Richard returned to the previous formation, with three columns parallel to the coast. The column nearest the beach comprised the baggage with infantry escorts, in the centre was the cavalry and on the left was a dense infantry screen, commanded by Count Henry of Champagne, which was

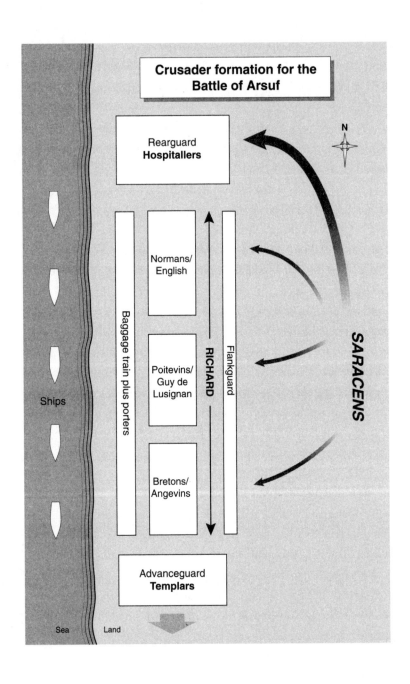

Crusader formation for the Battle of Arsuf

Rearguard **Hospitallers**

N

Normans/ English

Baggage train plus porters

Poitevins/ Guy de Lusignan

RICHARD

Flankguard

SARACENS

Ships

Bretons/ Angevins

Advanceguard **Templars**

Sea   Land

intended to protect the knights and consisted of a mixture of spearmen and crossbowmen.

The knights were divided into twelve squadrons, which were organised into five divisions. The Templars formed the advancee guard, followed by the Bretons and men of Anjou, then by the Poitevins, commanded by King Guy of Jerusalem and then by the Normans and English, who were escorting the Royal standard. Finally came the rearguard, provided on this day by the Hospitallers. As always, it is difficult to establish numbers with any degree of precision, but it appears that in overall terms the Saracens outnumbered the Crusaders by about two to one, although the imbalance in cavalry may well have been greater. A possible assessment is that the Crusaders numbered some 15,000–20,000 men, of which approximately 2,000–3,000 were knights, while facing them were about 25,000–30,000 Saracens, of which about 10,000 were cavalry.

Richard's orders to his troops were quite explicit. The task for the day was to reach the next way-station on the road to Jaffa, the deserted town of Arsuf, beating off Saracen attacks on the way. To achieve this, the infantry was ordered to keep the Saracens out of bow range of the cavalry, while the cavalry was under very strict orders to maintain the integrity of its formation and to continue its advance towards Arsuf – even in the face of the most severe provocation – unless specifically ordered to charge by Richard in person. It was made very clear that such an order would be given by Richard alone, using six simultaneous trumpets scattered in three pairs along the column. So tight-knit were the formations that one participant reported that: 'they kept together so closely, that an apple, if thrown, would not have fallen to the ground, without touching a man or a horse.' For a medieval army, command-and-control was exceptionally tight, as 'King Richard and the duke of Burgundy, with a chosen retinue of warriors, rode up and down, narrowly watching the position and manner of the Turks, to correct anything in their own troops, if they saw the occasion.'

The Crusaders set out just before dawn and the head of the column was approaching the outskirts of Arsuf at about 9 a.m. when Saladin unleashed the first attack:

> There appeared a large body of Turks, 10,000 strong, coming down on us at full charge, and throwing darts and arrows, as fast as they could, while they mingled their voices in one horrible yell. There followed after them an infernal race of men, of black colour, and bearing a suitable appellation, expressive of their blackness. With them also were Saracens, who live in the desert, called bedouins: they are a savage race of men, blacker than soot; they fought on foot, and carry a bow, quiver, and round shield, and are a light and active race ... Beyond them might be seen the well-arranged phalanxes of the Turks, with ensigns fixed to their lances, and standards and banners of separate distinctions.

This attack concentrated on the Crusaders' rearguard, where the infantry were soon being forced to march backwards as they endeavoured to hold off the enemy while also maintaining the advance towards Arsuf. Despite the unremitting pressure and the temperature – it was the hottest day anyone could remember – the Crusaders held firm. The loss of horses began to mount, although the unhorsed knights immediately joined the ranks of the infantry, and soon the Hospitallers were so hard pressed that they sent a message to Richard asking for permission to charge, but he declined, telling the messenger that they must continue as they were for the time being.

The pressure was steadily increased by the Saracens, with the Hospitallers forced up against the preceding division of Normans and English, but still they held. The Saracens, frustrated by their failure to pierce the Crusader column, suddenly attacked en masse, and this time the Grand

Master of the Hospitallers, Fra' Garnier de Nablus, galloped forward in person to request Richard's permission to charge to relieve the pressure. Once again Richard refused, telling him, somewhat enigmatically: 'Good Master, it is you who must sustain their attack; no one can be everywhere at once.' Things continued for a while longer, but the frustration among the Hospitallers eventually reached boiling point and two men – one of them the Grand Master himself – suddenly called on St George for aid and charged into the enemy ranks, a disobedience not only to Richard's orders, but also to the rules of the order, as the Grand Master was no doubt fully aware. At this, the infantry drew aside to open gaps through which other Hospitallers joined the charge, and units from the main body, seeing what was happening, followed suit.

Although this was in direct contravention of his orders, Richard, instead of trying to stop the charge, realised that the die was now cast and immediately ordered the trumpeters to sound the signal for the general charge.[9] Then, in his usual way, Richard immediately headed for the thickest of the fighting. By chance, the Crusaders caught the Saracen cavalry at a vulnerable moment, since many of them had dismounted, the better to aim their arrows and as a result the Crusader knights were able to catch them on foot, knocking many of them to the ground where they were quickly dispatched by the Crusader infantry, which was following closely behind.

The Saracens, who moments before had seemed to be having it all their own way, were now utterly demoralised and in the melee some even attacked their own men by mistake. The Saracen ranks broke, some running to the cliffs where they had no choice but to jump into the sea – a height of some 80 feet – while others climbed trees to escape the Crusaders' fury, but the majority simply fled as best they could. The Normans and the English did not join the general charge, but maintained their discipline, partly because they were responsible for the Royal standard, but also because they formed an uncommited reserve, ready for Richard to send wherever they were needed. So they moved slowly and under full control to a position in the immediate rear of the general fighting. Unfortunately, this move of the Royal banner caused a momentary misunderstanding as the Crusaders, perhaps tiring in the heat and fury of the battle, paused in their slaughter and turned to rally round it. Seeing what appeared to be temporary indecision in the Crusader ranks, Saladin rallied his men and counter-attacked, the advance being led by his household troops, some 700 strong, headed by a general (a relative of Saladin's) named Tekedmus. The fighting now became even more intense, with the Crusaders briefly on the defensive, but a knight named William de Barris led his company in a counter-attack, followed closely by Richard at the head of another squadron, and this was sufficient to turn matters in the Crusaders' favour once more.

The Saracens again withdrew and the Crusaders resumed their march towards Arsuf, but seeing this, another group of Saracen knights charged at the rearguard, whereupon Richard, leading a troop of only fifteen men, attacked the Saracens three times before they dispersed. Richard's final triumph of the day was to prevent the Crusader knights from charging too far after the enemy, something which they tended to do in the excitement of battle and which usually ended with them being cut off in small groups and killed or captured. The battle was now truly over and Saladin's army scattered to the shelter of the wooded hills.

According to estimates made on the spot, the Saracens had suffered 7,000 casualties, while the Crusaders had lost, at the very most, a tenth of that number. The loss most strongly felt by the Crusaders was that of James of Avesnes, a noted and popular warrior, who had led a group of French knights in the first charge, but was then isolated by Saracen horsemen and unhorsed. Together with three of his kinsmen, James killed fifteen Saracens before being killed himself.

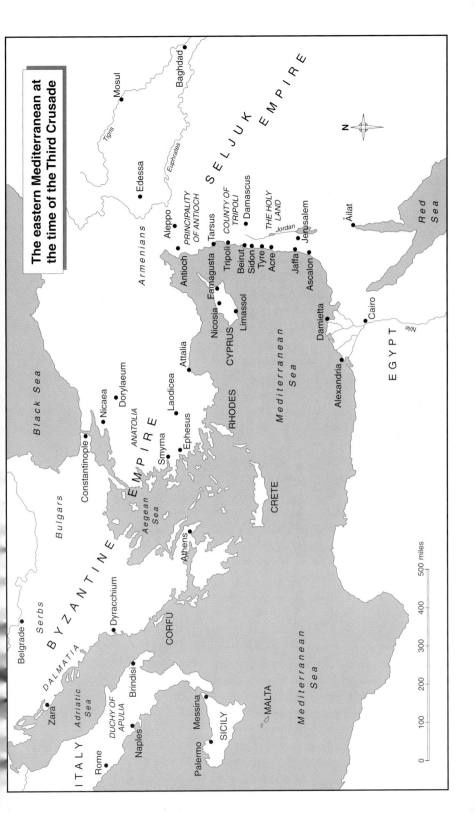

The eastern Mediterranean at the time of the Third Crusade

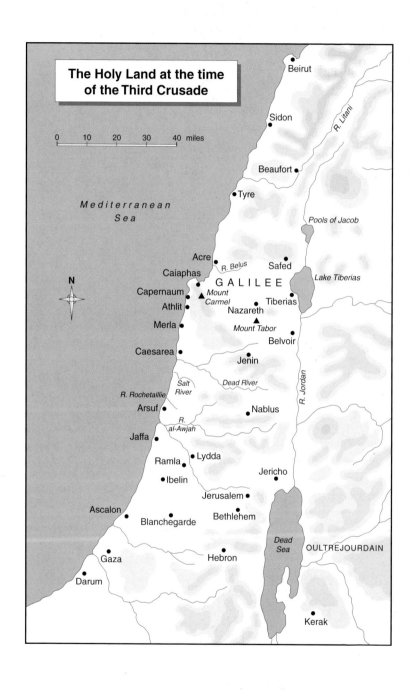

The Holy Land at the time of the Third Crusade

0   10   20   30   40 miles

Mediterranean Sea

Beirut

Sidon

R. Litani

Beaufort

Tyre

Pools of Jacob

Acre

R. Belus

Caiaphas

Safed

GALILEE

Lake Tiberias

N

Capernaum

Mount Carmel

Tiberias

Athlit

Nazareth

Merla

Mount Tabor

Belvoir

Caesarea

Jenin

Salt River

Dead River

R. Jordan

R. Rochetaillie

Arsuf

R. al-Awjah

Nablus

Jaffa

Ramla

Lydda

Ibelin

Jericho

Jerusalem

Ascalon

Bethlehem

Blanchegarde

Dead Sea

OULTREJOURDAIN

Gaza

Hebron

Darum

Kerak

Richard the Lionheart, King of England (1189–99). If ever there was a warrior king it was Richard. Only five months of his ten-year reign were spent in England, the remainder of his time being occupied with Crusading and defending his lands in France. (*Corbis*)

LEFT Saladin achieved a succession of victories over the Crusaders until Richard arrived in the Holy Land. Like Richard he was both a commander and a warrior, and the two leaders had great respect for one another. (*Corbis*)

ABOVE A medieval depiction of the massacre of the Saracen prisoners at Acre. In reality, it was a very bloody affair, involving hundreds of Crusader executioners. Despite the strategic rationale, the massacre left a stain on Richard's record. (*Peter Newark's Military Pictures*)

LEFT Richard and Philip of France enter Acre in 1191. The siege of the city had started before either arrived and between them they brought it to a successful conclusion. However Philip then returned home, leaving Richard to fight the Crusade. (*Peter Newark's Military Pictures*)

ABOVE Modern Acre (Akko). The outer walls of the ancient city have changed little since Richard's time and the Crusader siege positions were just to the left of this photograph. Many of the buildings inside the walls have been replaced over the centuries, but they remain just as crowded. (*Corbis*)

OPPOSITE TOP An eleventh-century Arab depiction of a Saracen army on the march. Such armies were always accompanied by musicians, drummers and a host of banners, all intended to encourage their own troops and to intimidate the enemy. (*Peter Newark's Military Pictures*)

RIGHT Richard was an extraordinarily courageous warrior, revelling in hand-to-hand combat and always to be found where the fighting was fiercest. Saladin's men did their best to either kill, capture or wound him, but never succeeded. (*Peter Newark's Military Pictures*)

The statue of Richard I, King of England, at Westminster Palace, London. Richard's achievements and character have been attacked for various reasons over the centuries, but there are very few to rival him as warrior, commander and strategist.
(*Peter Newark's Military Pictures*)

Day 18: Sunday 8 September

The following day, the Crusaders reorganised and recovered from the battle, while Saladin formed his troops nearby in the hope of a further engagement, but when the Crusaders did not move, he did not press them. A large search party was sent to the battlefield to recover the body of James of Avesnes, which was found and taken into the town where a burial service was conducted with Richard and Guy as the chief mourners. Meanwhile, Saladin sent a strong force to hold the River Arsuf, which reached the sea some 6 miles further south.

Day 19: Monday 9 September

Having recovered, the Crusaders set out on the morning of Day 19 with the Hospitallers leading and the Templars forming the rearguard. The Saracens had a strong force and engaged the Crusader column closely, but failed utterly in their attempts to persuade them to respond and break their ranks. The Saracens then took up a potential ambush position at the River al-Awjah, but when the Crusaders arrived there was only a brief skirmish before the Saracens faded away, leaving the Crusaders to make camp on both banks of the river. This lack of aggression was somewhat uncharacteristic of the Saracens, but it may be that Saladin realised that the Crusaders were now so close to Jaffa that there was no point in losing more men, or that the Saracen troops themselves were reluctant to fight.

Day 20: Tuesday 10 September

The Crusaders broke camp early on the morning of Day 20, their immediate goal now in sight, and by midday the leading elements were plodding wearily into Jaffa. The town had been so effectively demolished by Saladin's men that there was little shelter to be found, but the Crusaders made camp in the orchards surrounding the town and when the fleet arrived that afternoon, the audacious move was complete.

A Military Triumph

The entire operation was a major triumph for the Crusaders and their commander-in-chief. Richard had arrived at his strategic goal having fought countless skirmishes and a major battle – the latter at a time and place of the enemy's choice – and he remained master of the field, with his strategic, operational and tactical objectives all fulfilled. In addition, it was an important psychological victory for the Crusaders, and in particular, it confirmed Richard's ascendancy as a battlefield commander who was now regarded with the greatest respect not only by his own men, but also by his opponents, to whom he was known as 'Melek Ric' (King Richard).

In this operation Richard achieved a number of successes. It was the first time that the current generation of Crusaders had operated under a single and undisputed commander, who not only had a firm and clear operational plan, but also demonstrated the personality and authority to impose his wishes. Secondly, despite the lack of discipline inherent in all medieval armies and the added complications of this particular army's multinational composition and lack of training, he managed to retain a remarkable degree of central control. Finally, he had succeeded in welding his disparate force into a cohesive body in which all elements played their part.

One of the most noteworthy features of the operation was the importance that Richard attached to logistic support, which was divided into two main elements. Immediate support was provided by a baggage train of wagons, pack-horses and porters, whose protection was always given high priority. Further, this baggage train was fully integrated into the movement plan rather than left to follow on behind, as was all too usual in medieval armies. In addition to this, what would in modern times be termed 'second-line support' was provided by the sea train, composed of galleys, busses and barges, which kept pace with the advance in order to deliver provisions, supplies and reinforcements, and also to remove the sick and wounded.

Richard was very careful to operate well within the limits of his men's capabilities, keeping stages short – the longest march was 13 miles – and giving regular breaks and rest days. It is on record that several of the marches began at the 'third hour' suggesting a deliberate decision to take advantage of the coolest part of the day. Although not referred to by contemporary historians, getting such a large body of horsemen, infantry and wagons on the move in the dark must have been an extraordinarily difficult task, requiring a great degree of control and coordination.

The very dense marching formation and the slow pace would have had its disadvantages for those in the centre and at the rear, who must have suffered greatly from the heat, the press of men and horses jammed up against each other, and the generally unsavoury atmosphere. There was also the ever-present threat of the Saracens and the knowledge that if anyone dropped out they would assuredly be killed. However, the formation also kept everyone moving and ensured that the Saracens were presented with an almost impregnable target.

There was never any doubt that Richard was in full command of operations. His orders were absolutely firm and his authority was required for any variation. Each group within the army had a clearly defined commander, who was directly responsible to Richard. Richard also appointed nobles to serve as coordinators, with the task of riding up and down the column, ensuring control and ordering appropriate responses to minor attacks. Richard demonstrated not only leadership, but also personal courage, riding always at the point of maximum threat, and if action broke out elsewhere, heading straight for it and throwing himself into the melee.

All this meant that by 10 September 1191 Richard had totally achieved his strategic aim of moving both his army and his operational base from Acre to Jaffa, where he now stood with his army intact and threatening both Jerusalem and the road to Egypt. In addition, Richard had a secure supply line by sea and Saladin was left guessing as to what the Crusaders' next move might be.

CHAPTER 6

The First Attempt to Reach Jerusalem

The aim of the Third Crusade remained, as always, to retake Jerusalem, but following the hardships of the siege of Acre, the rigours of the march to Jaffa and the great victory at Arsuf, the army settled happily into a life of relative ease in Jaffa. The successes did, however, result in a further influx of reinforcements who had missed the march along the coast for one reason or another, mainly by indulging themselves in the fleshpots of Acre, while non-military pilgrims also arrived, eager to get yet another step nearer to Jerusalem. This was, however, counterbalanced by an outflow, partly of those who considered that they had now done enough and wanted to go home, but also of those who simply wanted to enjoy their share of the drinking dens and bordellos of Acre.

The Crusaders had arrived on 10 September 1191, but at the end of the month Richard moved them to a new campsite a little further away from Jaffa, which revealed just how considerable the reduction in numbers had been. As a result, Richard dispatched King Guy of Jerusalem to Acre to bring back the absentees, but he had little effect – as was usual with this weak man – so Richard went in person and his forceful personality and golden tongue were much more successful. He returned to Jaffa bringing not only rather more reinforcements than Guy had found, but also the two queens and the Maid of Cyprus (Isaac Comnenus's daughter). These administrative problems faded into insignificance, however, when compared with the major strategic problem of what to do next, and as happened all too frequently throughout the history of the Crusades, a major success was followed by months of dissension, discord and confusion, all of which combined to result in disappointment and, eventually, acute misery.

Saladin's Strategy

Saladin was now in a position of responding to the Crusaders and, as Richard had intended, the Saracen leader had to consider two main possibilities. The first was that the Crusaders would continue down the coast, using the same tactics as on their march from Acre to Jaffa, taking Ascalon and Damoun as they went, and then carry on to attack Egypt. The second possibility was that Richard would turn inland and head for Jerusalem, for which he had a choice of several possible routes. Furthermore, Saladin also had to worry about his own army, primarily because many of his troops were now very apprehensive of 'Melek Ric's' prowess, both as a general and as a warrior; indeed, the Saracen commander was concerned that if Richard was known to be heading for Ascalon, his fearsome reputation and, in particular, the incident of the massacre of the prisoners at Acre, might well cause the garrison to take to its heels before the Crusaders even arrived.

Having given the matter some consideration, Saladin decided to defend the approaches to Jerusalem by confining Richard to the coastal strip, and also destroy Ascalon, which was now the only port remaining open between Jaffa and Alexandria – this should deter Richard from invading Egypt. Never being one to confine his activities to a single front, Saladin also encouraged the various Crusader factions to fall out with each other, as well as doing his best to increase Richard's anxiety about threats to his interests back in Europe, especially where King Philip of France was concerned.

To implement the military side of his strategy, Saladin set up a blocking position on the Jaffa–Jerusalem road at Ramla, and established a covering force under his brother Saphadin at Ibelin, about 20 miles south of Jaffa, with instructions to harass the Crusaders at every opportunity. Saladin then personally led a small group to Ascalon where he expelled the townspeople and demolished the fortifications. Saladin, like Richard, worked alongside his men, consequently the place was flattened in just ten days. Saladin also paid a personal visit to Jerusalem (27–30 September), where he closely inspected the troops, the defences, and the state of provisions and military stores.

Saladin returned to Ramla on 30 September, and on 4 October he withdrew his army to a new position at Toron des Chevaliers, near Natroun, 10 miles south-east of Ramla and virtually half-way between Jaffa and Jerusalem. While they waited for Richard's next move, the Saracens demolished the watchtower that had been erected by the Hospitallers as part of their network to protect the pilgrims' routes to and from Jerusalem.

Richard's Options

As Saladin had surmised, Richard gave serious thought to an attack on Egypt, which would have been a brilliant strategic stroke and would undoubtedly have given the Saracens many problems, although whether it would have succeeded or not is a different matter. This idea was given greater prominence when some of the people expelled from Ascalon by Saladin reached Jaffa to tell how their town was being demolished, leading Richard to propose setting out at once to rescue what was left of Ascalon and then move on to the Nile delta. But to do so, he needed the whole-hearted agreement of the great majority of the army, and although he was the acknowledged and undisputed commander-in-chief, by no means did Richard have a free hand. Thus, as on several other occasions, he was obliged to call a meeting of the 'chiefs and leaders of the people' to decide whether to save Ascalon or to set out for Jerusalem. Having heard a variety of opinions Richard declared his own view, which was to save Ascalon, but, this was vehemently opposed by the Duke of Burgundy and the French nobles, who argued that it made more sense to restore Jaffa and then take the short route to Jerusalem. The majority was clearly with the French, leaving Richard no choice but to give in.

Richard's Foolhardy Exploits

A criticism levelled at Richard by many people, including by Saladin himself, was that despite his high responsibilities, he was frequently (some might even say, continuously) careless of his own safety. A typical incident took place on 29 September when he went hawking; after a good day's sport, he and his escort dismounted and appear to have dozed off in the heat. They then became victims of a classic entrapment, when a group of Saracen horsemen attacked them and then pretended flight, enticing the Crusaders into leaping onto their horses and, with Richard in the lead, charging in pursuit – straight into the ambush that had been prepared for them. As always, Richard fought like one possessed, but four Crusaders were killed and the king only escaped because one of the survivors of his party, William of Pratelles, shouted out in Arabic that he was 'Melek Ric' and allowed himself to be captured. When Richard returned to his camp, he was openly criticised by various people led by the Duke of Burgundy, for such foolhardy exploits.

Again, on 1 November, Richard was out riding near Ramla when he saw some Saracen scouts and rather than avoid action he charged straight at them, killing one, wounding several and putting the rest to flight. A more serious incident took place six days later when a group of Crusaders went out on a routine foray to obtain fodder for their horses. The party consisted of a group of esquires with an escort of Templars who were at work when a large group of Saracens charged down upon them. A fierce fight ensued, but one Crusader managed to escape and sought help from Richard who happened to be nearby. The king immediately dispatched a small party to assist the beleaguered group and prepared to follow, accompanied by only a small retinue. There then followed a classic exchange, as one of the escort told the king that they would be so heavily outnumbered that it would be 'better to let them perish than to expose your person and all Christendom to certain danger, whilst we have the power of escaping.' Richard's reaction summarised his entire philosophy, as he angrily told his more prudent follower, that if he neglected men he had sent forward with a promise to come after them, then he would lose all right to be called a king. He then dug his spurs into his horse's side and charged into the middle of the melee. A number of Saracens were killed and the Crusaders rescued, while Richard returned unharmed to the Crusader lines.

In addition to daylight attacks, the Saracens carried out many clandestine raids by night, mainly using 300 Arab thieves in Saladin's pay. Their task was to penetrate Crusader positions under cover of darkness in order to steal money, horses or other property, and, whenever possible, to kidnap or kill individuals. The victim would be woken to find a dagger at his throat and was immediately given the stark choice of being killed on the spot or being put into slavery.

Negotiations

On 3 October, Richard sought a non-military solution to the continuing conflict by renewing negotiations with Saphadin, Saladin's brother, sending Saladin a splendid horse to indicate the seriousness of his intentions. Richard's opening bid was to say that the war had gone on long enough and all that remained was for the Saracens to hand over the fragment of the Holy Cross they had captured at Hattin (something they had failed to do after the fall of Acre), and return both Jerusalem and all territory between the River Jordan and the Mediterranean to the Crusaders. Not surprisingly, Saladin rejected all three proposals, but Richard's next bid was to offer his sister Joanna, former Queen of Sicily, as bride to Saphadin, the two to reign jointly over the Kingdom of Jerusalem. Joanna would become a Muslim and would have the city as her royal seat, plus the cities of Acre, Jaffa and Ascalon. Unfortunately, Richard had neglected (or, perhaps, avoided) telling his sister of this plan, and when she heard of it Joanna was understandably furious and turned it down flat.

Richard conducted many negotiations with the Saracens and produced some far-fetched proposals in order to resolve the conflict, to ensure the retention of some sort of Crusader foothold in the Holy Land, and, above all, to enable him to leave the Crusade with his honour and reputation intact, so that he could return to resolve more important matters in his kingdom. However, this marriage proposal was the wildest of his ideas, and he should have known that no daughter of Eleanor of Aquitaine was likely to allow herself to be given away in such a high-handed manner. Richard may have been the master of many battlefields, but in this family skirmish his defeat was both rapid and complete.

Saladin was, as ever, ready to conduct negotiations with more than one Crusader faction and was also conducting quite separate negotiations with Conrad of Montferrat. The wily Conrad's aim was quite different from that of Richard, since, while the King of England was aiming to secure the Crusader position and obtain guaranteed access for pilgrims to Jerusalem, Conrad's aim was to get rid of the Crusader army and King Guy of Jerusalem, thus securing his own position as lord of Outremer. Conrad's opening offer, made when he initiated negotiations in October 1191, was that he would march on Acre and take it from the Crusaders, in return for which he wanted to be given Sidon and Beirut, and to have guaranteed retention of Tyre. The Saracen leadership seems to have felt little but contempt for Conrad, but dealt with him as it helped to promote internecine quarrels within the Crusader leadership.

Back to Campaigning

While these negotiations were going on, not only were both sides preparing to continue the war, but both also knew that the other was doing so; therefore, while Saladin's men were demolishing various fortifications, Richard's men were repairing others. In addition, Richard also undertook a first cautious probe inland, leaving a strong garrison at Jaffa and taking the remainder of his army to repair Casal des Plains and Casal Maen, the nearest two of the strongholds which had been built to protect the road to Jerusalem.

The Crusader army arrived at Casal Maen on 30 October 1191 and by December life had become very miserable as the weather turned ever colder and wetter; the men were dirty, everything was permanently damp, and there was a great deal of sickness. Nevertheless, by late December it was clear that the Crusaders intended to move on Jerusalem, so Saladin carried out a tactical withdrawal, continuing to destroy fortresses and outlying fortifications as he did so, while Richard advanced to Beit-Nuba (Bethnoble), which was reached on 3 January 1192. They were now only 12 miles from Jerusalem, but the weather was appalling, with strong winds and low temperatures, accompanied by rain, sleet or snow, which frequently turned campsites into quagmires. Knights' armour and swords started to rust, while food decayed more quickly than usual and clothing rotted. All this, coupled with a steady reduction in numbers due to departures and desertions, made the outlook increasingly bleak, although many remained buoyed up in anticipation of finally reaching Jerusalem.

Conditions in the Crusader camp went from bad to worse, morale plummeted and eventually there was a general feeling that enough was enough and on about 11 or 12 January another high-level council was held at which those with detailed local knowledge – the Hospitallers, Templars and those who had made their home in the Holy Land – were asked to examine the problems and then to express an opinion on what should be done. The first problem was that the Saracens were making determined and sustained attacks on the lines of communication between Jaffa and the army inland. The second problem was that when Richard asked those with local knowledge to draw a map of Jerusalem, on examination he noticed the extent of the walls, which meant that he would have to spread his men very thinly around the city to prevent Saracen supplies getting in. Worse, if those in the city made a foray they could easily penetrate the thin screen of attackers and Richard would not have a reserve with which to come to their support, unless he created a gap elsewhere. Having considered these factors in combination with the appalling weather, the council unanimously recommended to the king that the present advance on Jerusalem should be abandoned and that the army should return to the coast and rebuild Ascalon. This would then serve as an advance post from which Saracen caravans from Egypt to Jerusalem could be attacked (which was pretty much what Richard had proposed several months earlier).

When the troops were told of this decision they were extremely despondent. Many were undoubtedly motivated by genuine religious zeal and had been sustained throughout their recent hardships by the prospect of reaching the Holy City. From Richard's viewpoint these were somewhat dangerous people, since he knew that having reached the Holy City many of them would then simply return home, considering their duty done, leaving the Crusader army seriously weakened and unable to withstand the inevitable Saracen counter-attack. There were also, unavoidably, others who wanted to reach Jerusalem for a more mundane reason – a successful siege always meant serious booty.

In fact, the weather conditions at Jerusalem were even worse than the Crusaders were experiencing, with heavy snow and hail mixed with flash-floods so severe that mules and horses were swept away. When they learned of this later, some Crusaders felt that they should have taken advantage of the bad weather and poor Saracen morale to lay siege to Jerusalem, overlooking the fact that the bad weather would have affected both sides equally. Indeed, the Crusaders were themselves in bad shape, with sickness rampant and many unable to carry their own rations, while the horses and mules were constantly collapsing through hunger and exhaustion.

Seeing all this, Richard had the sick brought together and escorted down to Ramla, and thence to Jaffa, and on 13 January 1192 the army started to withdraw to Ascalon, via Ibelin. Their misery continued, with the weather so bad that animals fell into the mud, were unable to get up and then died, while much of the provisions were ruined by water. As they approached the coast, the Duke of Burgundy and most of the French contingent separated from the army; some going on to Jaffa, some to Acre, others went even further northwards to throw in their lot with Conrad of Montferrat at Tyre, while the balance, led by the duke, went to Casel des Plains just outside Jaffa.

Meanwhile, the main body of the army struggled on towards Ascalon, which they reached on 20 January, but their suffering was then compounded when the weather became even worse, with snow and hail beating in their faces. Throughout all this and despite the conditions, the Saracens remained at the Crusaders' heels, attacking whenever the slightest opportunity showed itself, and making it unsafe to go foraging. To cap all this misery, when the Crusaders reached Ascalon they found it levelled by the Saracens and the port facilities so damaged that it was eight days before the supply ships could enter the harbour with desperately needed food.

On the other side, the marauding Saracens snapping at the Crusaders' heels were, in fact, merely a screen, because further back many of Saladin's men, who had now been on campaign continuously for four years, were becoming restive. Consequently, Saladin was actually quite relieved for the Crusaders to be back on the coast, as he then felt sufficiently confident to allow many of his men to go on leave until May.

Richard managed to persuade the Duke of Burgundy and some of the French to rejoin him, although they only agreed to stay until Easter, which fell on 5 April that year. All now concentrated on rebuilding Ascalon, with everyone taking part, whether nobles or soldiers, priests or laymen, princes or servants, and the progress was much more rapid than they had dared hope. Richard was not only in control, allotting men tasks, but at every opportunity he also worked alongside them, heaving and carrying with the best.

Richard also conducted his own reconnaissances, one of which involved a visit to the Saracen-held castle at Darum, approximately 20 miles to the south, with a view to working out how he could take it. By chance, he and his escort arrived at the same time as a Saracen column taking 1,000 Christian captives on their way to Egypt and slavery, but as soon as the Saracen escort caught sight of Melek Ric's banner they promptly abandoned their charges and fled into the fortress. Richard released the captives and then went looking for any Saracens prepared to fight him; he killed a few, capturing twenty to be held as hostages, as well as a large number of horses, and returned to Ascalon after a most successful day.

Crusader Quarrels

When not fighting the Saracens, one of the Crusaders' most time-consuming activities was quarrelling with each other and they now indulged in several particularly bruising rounds. When King Philip of France left the Holy Land at the end of July 1191 he had appointed the Duke of Burgundy as commander of the French contingent, but left him no money, only instructions to use the ransom payments due on the prisoners who had been captured when Acre fell. At the time, Richard had lent Burgundy a large sum on the surety of the ransom, but when virtually the entire Saracen garrison was killed, Burgundy's means of repayment disappeared as well. Thus, not only had Burgundy not repaid Richard, but his soldiers had not been paid for some time either, and now he was bankrupt. The proud duke was left with no alternative but to approach Richard for yet more money, but the king had had enough and refused, whereupon Burgundy took umbrage and stormed off to Acre, accompanied, somewhat surprisingly, by his still unpaid soldiers.

When the French reached Acre they found the city in turmoil because the Genoese, who by now supported Conrad of Montferrat, had fallen out with the Pisans, who favoured King Guy – a quarrel which had progressed through arguments and fistfights to actual bloodshed. When the French arrived outside the city they immediately took the side of the Genoese, whereupon the Pisans attacked the column, stabbed the duke's horse and brought him to the ground before withdrawing back into the city and locking the gates, at which the duke sent a messenger to Conrad in Tyre, pleading for help. Learning of the latter's imminent arrival, the Pisans sent word of their plight to Richard, who happened to be at Caesarea on his way north for a meeting with Conrad. The king immediately hurried to Acre and such was his reputation, that on hearing of his approach Conrad and his men, accompanied by the Duke of Burgundy and the Frenchmen, all retreated to Tyre. When Richard rode into Acre on 1 April 1192, he found only the original population and calling them together, he managed to clear up all the issues between the various parties and thus restore tranquillity in the city.

With one crisis resolved, Richard turned to another and renewed his invitation to Conrad to meet him, as he had promised. The conference duly took place at a fortress called Ymbric, some miles north of Acre and they had a very long discussion, but to no effect, as a result of which Richard returned to his army at Ascalon and called an assembly of 'the leaders and more discreet men of the army'. This body advised Richard that Conrad, by his behaviour, had forfeited the right to be the next king of Jerusalem and that he should also forgo all his revenues. This ended in a yet wider rift between the French and Conrad on one side and Richard and the remainder of the army on the other, and Conrad endeavoured to persuade all the remaining French to leave Richard's army at Ascalon and join him at Tyre. Richard remained at Ascalon with his army for the Easter celebrations, during which he knighted Saphadin's son, a unique honour for a Muslim.

Constant Skirmishing

Despite the apparent inactivity during this period, there continued to be constant minor engagements between the two sides, with foraging parties being particularly popular targets, as the two sides searched ever more widely for supplies, particularly fodder for their horses and wood for their fires. Each of these skirmishes usually resulted in a few deaths and prisoners, and served to keep everyone on their toes, but without affecting the overall situation. Three of these events will serve to set the tone.

In the first, Robert de Harcourt, Earl of Leicester (1156–1205), played a major role, while King Richard somehow managed to miss the excitement. The conflict occurred in December 1191, when a large body of Turkish cavalry, probably about 100–150 strong, rode towards the Crusader position, shouting taunts at their enemy. It so happened that the Earl of Leicester was nearby with a few of his knights, and taking offence, three of them charged the enemy, who fled. However, when the Saracens saw that their nearest pursuers were three knights who had outstripped their comrades, they turned and quickly captured them.

The Earl and the remainder of his train were infuriated by this and threw themselves at the Saracens in order to rescue their comrades. As they fought, the Saracens gradually withdrew, pulling back across a river, still engaged in hand-to-hand fighting. As usual, the main Saracen tactic was to unhorse their opponents and they managed to knock the earl into the river; his horse escaped, but the weight of his armour almost caused him to drown before he managed to get to his feet. One of the Crusaders, Robert de Newbury, considered his liege lord's safety of far greater importance than his own and leapt into the water, insisting that the earl take his horse. Meanwhile, more Saracens arrived on the scene and eventually the few surviving Crusaders were defenceless and reduced to lying across their horses' necks while the enemy belaboured them with iron maces, until, tiring of this activity, the Saracens started to lead their prisoners away. The noise of the conflict had, however, been heard in the Crusader camp, where a rescue party was quickly mobilised, charging forward to join the fray. There then followed a general melee, in which the earl lost his second horse, but mounted a third and continued fighting. Eventually the Saracens withdrew and the exhausted Crusaders returned to their own camp.

Although the Saracens regularly succeeded in such tactics, they did not always have the initiative. On Friday 27 March 1192, for example, a group of young knights sortied from Jaffa in the direction of Mirabel (about 10 miles east-north-east from Jaffa), in the course of which they slew thirty Saracens, captured fifty more, and brought back many cattle and much booty. They gave the due amount to the governor and sold the remainder.

The following day, Saturday 28 March, another group of knights from Ascalon sortied south as far as Darum and rounded up some 200 Saracen men, women and children, as well as many horses and cattle.

Conclusions

Richard conducted this phase of his campaign with great prudence. His personal inclination was to carry on down the coast, which would give the army guaranteed logistical support from the sea for delivery of supplies and reinforcements, as well as the removal of the sick and wounded. When the council decided that the army was to go to Jerusalem instead, he complied but proceeded with great circumspection, extending his line carefully and slowly, and consolidating after each forward step. As a result, this was not a great and inexorable march on Jerusalem, on the lines of the move from Acre to Jaffa, but rather a very cautious move forward; indeed it took two months to reach their farthest point, Beit-Nuba, which was only 25 miles from Jaffa. There is no doubt that the very bad weather played a significant role in all this, although it is not clear whether the conditions were worse than usual or whether the locally-domiciled Crusaders did not make the possibility of poor weather clear; perhaps, however, they did so and were ignored.

Thus, the great success of the march from Acre to Jaffa had been offset by the very unsuccessful attempt to reach Jerusalem. Unfortunately, this had brought the split between the French and the English camps into the open, while Conrad of Montferrat continued to act as a gad-fly, unpredictable, very annoying and diverting the attention of the main players. So, early February 1192 found the Crusaders back on the coast where the great question was, what were they to do next?

CHAPTER 7

Interlude

When Richard announced the findings of the council concerning Conrad – that he had not only forfeited the right to be the next king of Jerusalem, but would also forgo his share of the royal revenues – the rift between the French and Conrad on one side and Richard and the remainder of his army on the other widened even further. Conrad responded by sending messengers to persuade the remaining 700 French knights to leave Richard's army at Ascalon and join him and the Duke of Burgundy at Tyre. These knights felt that their oath of allegiance obliged them to obey and on Thursday 2 April 1192, the day after his return to Ascalon, their leaders met Richard and asked him to honour the previous bargain, not only to release them but also to provide an escort to see them safely on their way. This Richard did, albeit with great reluctance, and, not surprisingly, Saladin was delighted to see the Crusader army splitting up into factions.

Despite this serious set-back, Richard celebrated Easter Sunday, which fell on 5 April, in great style at Ascalon, laying on a magnificent entertainment, which was open to all. However, it was only a brief, if generous, break: all had to return to work on the city walls the following day and on 7 April Richard set out to reconnoitre the fortress of Darum, which he walked around to assess its weaknesses.

Later that week Richard received yet another blow, this time in the form of a letter from the Prior of Hereford in England, who described the deteriorating situation back home. The king's brother, Earl John, was causing great distress and, among other things, had expelled the chancellor and usurped the royal revenues. Having mulled over the news, Richard called the leaders of the army together and told them what he had learned, informing them that he had decided to return home, but would leave behind 300 knights and 2,000 selected foot soldiers, all to be paid for at his expense and all to be volunteers.

Unfortunately for Richard, this mention of the very real possibility of his departure inevitably reopened the question of who would assume the command when he left and meant that the question of who should be the king of Jerusalem had to be re-examined yet again. Thus, shortly after Easter he reconvened the council of his chief advisers at Ascalon and instructed them to resolve the question once and for all. As before, the only two candidates were Guy of Lusignan and Conrad of Montferrat, and after considerable discussion and some deep heart-searching all involved unanimously recommended Conrad as being 'much better able to defend the country than any other they could choose'.

Richard may have felt some personal regret that Guy, the man he had supported up till now (and his kinsman) had not been recommended. However, he seems to have been enough of a pragmatist to realise that Conrad was by far the stronger character, with a powerful will, fired by ambition, and a renowned fighter – everything, in other words, that Guy was not. This was one occasion when Richard, with some justice, might have expressed indignation at the change of heart, but instead he 'censured them in gentle terms for their fickleness, for they had before this often detracted from the character and good qualities of the marquis [Conrad]'.

When he announced his agreement the choice was greeted with acclaim and it appeared that this most vexatious question had, at long last, been resolved. Thus, Count Henry of Champagne, accompanied by a high-ranking delegation, was dispatched to Tyre to convey the good news to Conrad and to summon him to join Richard at Ascalon. But, as seemed to be the inevitable fate of the Third Crusade, every time a solution to a problem appeared to be in sight, some totally unexpected event set all back to nought again – and the election of Conrad as king was no exception.

The Death of Conrad

Having delivered his message, which gave rise to great delight to Conrad, his court and the people of Tyre, Count Henry set off to rejoin Richard, leaving the new king to organise what would doubtless be a triumphant journey to join Richard for the planned march on Jerusalem. Arrangements were well in hand when, in the late afternoon of 27 April 1192, Conrad was awaiting the return of his wife, Isabella, from the baths, so that they could have supper together. For some reason she was delayed and when she failed to appear, hunger got the better of Conrad and, accompanied by two knights, he went to the house of his friend, the Bishop of Beauvais, only to discover that the bishop had already eaten. Naturally, the bishop offered to provide a meal, but Conrad decided to return home again, his route taking him down a narrow street, where he approached two young men who were sitting, one against either wall.

The two men stood as he approached and Conrad must have recognised them as they had been members of his entourage for some considerable time. As he reached them, one of them held out a letter and Conrad stopped his horse to reach down to accept it, whereupon the man with the letter stabbed upwards with a hidden knife, while the other leapt onto the horse and stabbed their victim in the back. Conrad fell to the ground and died shortly afterwards. One of the murderers was killed on the spot and the other was very brutally tortured, during which he confessed that he and his comrade were Assassins and had been sent by the 'Old Man of the Mountains'; then he too was dispatched. There were rumours, both at the time and since, that Richard was implicated in the murder of Conrad, and in order to refute this it is necessary to describe some of the background.

The two murderers were almost certainly members of an Islamic military order, whose popular Arabic name was *hashishiyyin*, supposedly because they carried out their attacks while under the influence of drugs. The original group never numbered more than a few hundred and carried out a relatively small number of killings between about 1090 AD and 1256 AD, but the majority of their victims were persons of considerable importance, and with only a very few exceptions, Muslims. So powerful was their influence, however, and so audacious their acts, that to this day almost every political murder anywhere in the world is designated an 'assassination' and its perpetrator, whatever his or her motive or religious beliefs, is named an 'assassin'.

The group had its origins in the events following the death of the Prophet Mohammed in 632 AD, when his followers split into Sunnis, who believed that the elected caliphs of Baghdad were the rightful successors, and Shias, who traced authority through the *imams* (priests) descended from the Prophet through his daughter Fatimah. The situation was further complicated when the sixth Shia imam died in 765 AD, at which point the Shias themselves split into two, with one group retaining the name Shia, while the second became known as the Ismailis. The latter became very powerful, establishing the Fatimid caliphate, which ruled Egypt and Tunisia until toppled by the Sunni warrior leader, Saladin, in 1171.

A mainstream Shia, a Persian named Hassan as-Sabah, converted to Ismaili in 1072 but later established his own sect and dispatched teachers to win converts. He set up his base in a virtually impregnable castle known as the Eagle's Nest near the northern Persian city of Daylam, where he spent most of his time in religious contemplation and study, but he also founded a small group of the most dedicated of his followers as an elite corps of killers, who waged war by carefully staged and skilfully carried out murders of particular individuals. Hassan's primary targets were other Muslim leaders, his first significant victim being Nizar al-Mulk, the Grand Vizier of Persia, while another was the Prince of Emessa, who was murdered while en route to attack the invading Crusaders in 1102. These killings were not seen as random acts of murder, but as carefully controlled and executed religious deeds, whose sanctity was ensured because the dagger used in the deed had always been blessed by Grand Master Hassan for the murder of that particular individual.

Since they had to dispatch their victim by a blow from a dagger, the Assassins were, of necessity, particularly adept at disguising themselves, so that they could get close to their intended targets without arousing suspicion. They were helped in this by the fact that time was not a factor – there was no question of hurry and some murders took years to achieve. Hassan demanded absolute loyalty from his followers and was utterly ruthless. He demonstrated this on several recorded occasions by ordering followers to commit immediate suicide to prove their loyalty. He also ordered the deaths of several of his sons; one for breaking the rule that banned drinking, another because he plotted the death of another Assassin.

Hassan died in 1124 and his policies were continued more or less unchanged by the next two leaders of his group. Under these men, a second Persian Grand Vizier was murdered in his own stables in 1127, the Fatimid caliph was murdered in Cairo in 1130 and the Caliph of Baghdad in 1139. All these three victims were very important people and aware of the danger, but despite the protection of numerous guards they were unable to avoid the Assassin's dagger.

The fourth Grand Master, Hassan II, took office in 1162 and then tried to convert the Assassin beliefs into a new and separate religion, independent of Islam, but this was too much and he became a victim of his own followers, being murdered by his brother-in-law in 1166. The movement returned to its Islamic beliefs, while still maintaining the independence established by the original Grand Master, but, mainly through the influences of geography and distance, it split into two semi-autonomous wings. One of these, the Persian wing, was still based in the original stronghold of Alamut, but the other, which became far more closely involved with the Crusaders, was located in Syria, being based in the mountains south of Antioch at the castle of Kahf, which the Assassins had bought from the local emir in 1135. This Syrian wing was led from 1162 to 1192 by Sinan ibn Salman ibn Mohammed, who allegedly turned to killing for money rather than for purely religious reasons. He exercised a rule of terror from his stronghold and became known to the Crusaders as 'the Old Man of the Mountains'.[10]

Despite the depredations of the Crusaders, the Assassins still concentrated most of their efforts on fellow Muslims, Sinan twice sending men to kill Saladin, but they failed and Saladin responded by raiding Ismaili territory. According to many reports, Saladin was persuaded to desist when, despite the most stringent safety precautions, he woke one morning to find a poisoned dagger lying on his pillow, placed there as a warning.

The first known Crusader victim was Count Raymond II of Tripoli who, in 1152, was riding through the city gate when he was attacked by a group of Assassins, who killed him and two of his escorts, and then disappeared, never to be caught. The attack on Conrad took place forty years later and the motive behind it remains one of history's great mysteries. There seems little doubt that the two killers were members of the Assassins. Most sources also agree that both had been members of Conrad's entourage for 'some time', but without being more specific, and this does not resolve the two questions of who ordered them to carry out the deed and why. Saladin was known to consider Conrad a real long-term threat, since Richard was bound to leave the Holy Land to return to his kingdom, whereas Conrad clearly had every intention of remaining, especially as he was now the king-elect of Jerusalem.[11] However, Saladin himself had been an intended victim of the Assassins on several occasions and it seems improbable that he would have been in a position to persuade the 'Old Man of the Mountains' to take on what would today be termed a contract killing of a third party.

There have been suggestions that Richard was responsible. Curiously, Saladin's biographer, Bahā' al-Dīn, reports the incident and mentions that the two men, when questioned, said that the King of England had ordered it, but expresses no opinion himself as to who was responsible. Conrad had certainly caused Richard considerable problems throughout his stay in the Holy Land, even though Richard had gone out of his way to accommodate him. Richard, however, was increasingly desperate to return home and, with the election of Conrad as king, there was at last a man of action to take over the campaign and enable him to depart sooner rather than later. Nor does it seem likely that Richard had Conrad killed in order to install Count Henry, since Henry was acclaimed by the people of Tyre before Richard knew of Conrad's death, and Richard then took several days to agree to the proposal that Henry should both become king and wed the widowed Isabella. That leaves the 'Old Man of the Mountains' himself – several reports state that he was furious with Conrad over a previous incident in which the latter had interfered with one of Sinan's ships, purloined its cargo, and when the merchants objected, had them drowned.

Aftermath

The bulk of the French contingent had previously made its way to Tyre, where they were camped in tents outside the walls, and led by their commander, the Duke of Burgundy, they now attempted to enter the city to hold it 'in trust' for King Philip of France. Isabella, however, refused to allow them in, stating that Conrad, with his dying breath, had ordered her to hand it over only to Richard. Meanwhile, Count Henry was on his way back to join Richard and was at Acre when he was overtaken by a messenger and told of Conrad's death. Henry immediately retraced his steps to Tyre, presumably in order to discover for himself what had happened and then report it to Richard, but on his arrival the populace hailed him as the only suitable man to wed Conrad's widow and thus become the new King of Jerusalem.

Henry appears to have been genuinely taken by surprise by this development and told his supporters that the matter must be referred to Richard. When the latter was consulted, he agreed that Henry should be King of Jerusalem but had severe reservations about a marriage to Isabella who, he said (and most agreed with him), was tainted by the extremely questionable annulment of her first marriage, which had made her second marriage to Conrad of very doubtful legality and would further taint a third ceremony. Henry was a very suitable candidate for the crown, not least because he was the nephew of both the English and French kings, and had acquitted himself well in the fighting, but Richard declined to give a direction on whether or not he should marry the widow. When this reply was relayed to Henry at Tyre he appears to have hesitated, but under pressure from the French and following a personal appeal from Isabella, he decided to marry her, the wedding taking place on 5 May 1192. In fact, since Isabella was the only descendant of Jerusalem's blood royal, had Henry become king without marrying her, he would have been repeatedly challenged, leading to yet more quarrels.

Darum

As described on page 117 Richard had already conducted a personal reconnaissance of Darum and he now decided to take it. His message to Henry to accept the kingship had included a request to bring all the troops he could find to assist in this project, but Richard, who was described in a classic understatement by a contemporary as a man 'who hated delay', decided to go ahead on his own. He accordingly dispatched his siege train by sea and set out with the main body of the army by land, arriving at Darum on Sunday 17 May.

The fortress of Darum had sixteen towers and a citadel, was surrounded by a deep ditch, and was manned by a substantial and well-equipped garrison. When Richard arrived, he had insufficient men even to surround the fortress and the Saracens sortied out to frighten these impudent foreigners, but when Richard and his men proved to be unimpressed, they withdrew inside and barricaded the entrances. Shortly afterwards, the ships arrived carrying the dismantled siege engines, but as the beach shelved very gently the ships could not approach the shore too closely, so Richard mobilised his entire army and whether king, prince, noble or ordinary soldier, all laboured to bring the parts of the machines ashore, carry them a mile inland to the required place and then assemble them. As soon as they were ready the engines were put to use, operating around the clock, with Richard being personally in command of one that was attacking the citadel.

The following day Richard set the miners to work. They were mercenaries from Aleppo, who had been serving the Muslims in Acre, but who transferred their allegiance to their new paymaster when the city fell. Meanwhile, the Crusaders' siege engines were used collectively to destroy a Saracen mangonel on the citadel. They then switched targets to the fortress gate and this too was destroyed, whereupon, the garrison commander, fearful of Richard's ruthless reputation, sent an embassy with an offer to surrender the fort and its contents, subject only to the lives of the garrison being spared. Richard dismissed them brusquely with instructions to the Saracens to defend themselves properly.

Shortly afterwards one of the towers, undermined by the miners and hit repeatedly by stones, collapsed and the Saracens struggled to retire into the citadel, suffering numerous casualties in the process. They also cut the sinews of their horses, to prevent them being of use to the Crusaders, a wanton act of cruelty to animals, which aroused the Crusaders' ire far more than the killing of humans.

The Crusaders poured into the fortress, killing anyone they could find, and raised their banners on the ramparts, before turning their attention to the citadel. At this, the garrison, still some 300 strong, capitulated, only five days after Richard's arrival. Henry and the Duke of Burgundy arrived shortly afterwards; they were too late, but Richard immediately handed the fortress over to Henry, and then, having established a Crusader garrison, they all departed on Monday 25 May for Ascalon. On the way, they heard that a Saracen force was repairing the defences of a nearby abandoned fort, Majdal Yaba, and Richard immediately led a force to attack them, but on hearing of the approach of the dreaded 'Melek Ric' the Saracens fled.

At this juncture (i.e. about 30 May 1192) another emissary arrived from England, to tell the king of the country's desperate situation, where his younger brother John was clearly about to attempt to take over. Obviously, Richard was deeply troubled by this, and news of the message quickly spread throughout the army. Once again a council was held, attended by the leaders of the Angevin, English, French, Maine, Norman and Poitevin contingents, and for once they all agreed: they would advance on Jerusalem without delay, whether King Richard stayed with them or returned home to England. What is not recorded, however, is quite who would have led them if Richard had left, but this became irrelevant when a herald announced on 4 June 1192 that the king had decided to remain with them in the Holy Land until the following Easter (i.e. 28 March 1193) and that everyone was to prepare to march on Jerusalem.

CHAPTER 8

Jerusalem – The Second Attempt

Richard's announcement of the impending assault on Jerusalem was greeted with great enthusiasm throughout the army and all immediately made ready to march, the foot soldiers even declaring that they were prepared to carry one month's supplies instead of the usual ten days'. The army left its camp outside Ascalon on Sunday 7 June and although progress was slow because of the heat, the enthusiasm was undimmed and the camaraderie such that the richer members made their spare horses and mules available to the poorer to ease their task. They made good progress, reaching Blanchegarde (Tell al-Safiya) that evening and staying there for two nights, even though two of their number were killed by snakes on the first night.

On 9 June, the army moved on to Toron des Chevaliers, an observation post constructed by the Templars some years previously, where during the night, a group of fourteen Saracen infiltrators were captured trying to get inside the Crusader camp. Next day the army moved again, reaching Casel Arnaldi, where on 11 June the French contingent under the Duke of Burgundy rejoined them. The following day they moved on to Beit-Nuba, where they remained for some time awaiting the return of Count Henry, who had been sent by Richard on one of the periodic trips to Acre to round-up the many men known to be wasting their time there. In addition, supply convoys were moving up the road from Jaffa, bringing the provisions and stores necessary to establish the place as a forward depot for the final attack on Jerusalem.

Richard, of course, was not the man to wait on events and that night (11/12 June) a spy arrived to tell him that there was a party of Saracens nearby lying in ambush at the Pool of Emmaus, waiting to catch any unwary Crusaders. Richard immediately assembled a small party and they swooped on the would-be ambushers at dawn, killing twenty, capturing one, whom they recognised as Saladin's herald, and seizing camels and horses, including some of the famous and greatly valued Turcomans. A number of Saracens fled and Richard set off in pursuit; he managed to catch one and as he paused after killing him he looked up and saw the Holy City, Jerusalem, in the distance – the only time he was ever to set eyes on his goal.

While Richard was thus engaged, a raiding party of 200 Saracens caused considerable confusion in the army's campsite at Beit-Nuba. The incident started when the Saracens caught two men who had left the main position in search of fodder for their mules and who managed to shout a warning before they were killed. As before, the Saracen tactic rapidly sucked in increasing numbers of Crusaders. First came a group of French, Templars and Hospitallers who engaged the Saracens, but were starting to get the worst of it, when a further party of Frenchmen arrived, but it was only when the Bishop of Salisbury arrived with several hundred men that the Saracens were forced to withdraw. Meanwhile, news of Richard's proximity had reached the Saracens in Jerusalem and something approaching panic seems to have seized the garrison and they all made preparations to leave, even Saladin calling for a speedy mount to be held ready for his use.

On 17 June, a supply convoy left Jaffa with a heavy escort which should have been commanded by Count Henry of Champagne – which indicates just how important such a task was considered to be – but in his absence it was commanded by Frederick de Viana. The convoy had to pass near Ramla where a Saracen cavalry unit descended on the rear, arriving with such violence that a number of knights were unhorsed, while several took to their heels. In the closequarter fighting the Saracens used their iron clubs to great effect, seriously wounding a number of knights. Fortunately, reinforcement arrived, led by the Earl of Leicester, altering the balance firmly in the Crusaders' favour and the Saracens withdrew.

On Monday 22 June, a hermit came to see King Richard, informing him that he possessed a piece of the True Cross, hidden in a secret place, which he was prepared to reveal to the king. To the joy of the army, which set great store by such things, this relic was duly recovered, although once the rejoicing was over the mood swung to one of depression as the army continued to wait while still only a short distance from Jerusalem.

Another Conference

Once again there was a discussion over what to do next, with the French arguing loudly for an immediate advance on Jerusalem. Richard's reply is worth quoting in full:

> You will not find me leading the people in such a way as to lay myself open to reprehension or shame. Truly it would be the mark of an unwary man if I were to lend myself to any such folly. But, if you see fit to attack Jerusalem, I will not desert you; I will be your comrade though not your lord; I will follow but I will not lead. Saladin knows everything

that is done in our army, he knows our capacity and our strength. We are far from the coast, and if Saladin should come down into the plain of Ramla with his host and cut off our provisions by guarding the ways [i.e. cutting the route Jaffa–Beit-Nuba–Ramla] would not this, I ask you, be our utter ruin? Then, however, it would be too late for repentance. Besides, the circuit [circumference] of Jerusalem, so far as we hear, is very large, and if our little host were to attempt to close it on every side, our numbers would not suffice for the siege and the protection of those who bring up our stores. Besides, if I were to sanction any such imprudence while I was leader, and if any misfortune befell us, I alone should be charged with rashness, and be reckoned responsible for the danger of all. Moreover I know for certain that there are some here (and in France too) who are most eager for me to act rashly, and lay myself open to some dishonouring charge. For these reasons I do not think fit to show any hurry in the conduct of such difficult affairs. Besides we and our people are strangers, entirely ignorant of the district, its roads and its passes ... Therefore I think it better to proceed on the advice of the natives who, we may be sure, are eager to get back to their old possessions, and who know the country. It seems fit to follow the advice of the Templars and the Hospitallers – as to whether we shall advance to the siege of Jerusalem or to [be]siege Babylon [Cairo][12], Beirut, or Damascus. If we adopt their advice our army will no longer be, as it now is, torn apart by such great dissensions.

The decision was of such gravity and of such fundamental importance to every man in the army that a very formal decision-making process was established with a jury of twenty men, consisting of 'five Templars, five Hospitallers, five native Syrians belonging to the land, and five French nobles', but not, it should be noted, any representatives of Richard's realms, because they would follow their king. After lengthy consideration the committee of twenty concluded that the best course was to head for Egypt and lay siege to Cairo, to which the French contingent immediately 'offered a persistent opposition, declaring that they would not move except against Jerusalem'; and this, despite the fact that they had agreed to the procedure and five of their leaders had been on the committee.

Richard found himself once again faced by the total intransigence of the French. He tried to break the log-jam by offering the French the loan of his entire fleet to help them in the march to Cairo and offered to finance 700 knights and 2,000 sergeants, and to lend money as needed. It was to no avail, so, true to his word, he said that he would go to the siege of Jerusalem, but only as commander of his own subjects, and called his men together to decide how they would accomplish this.

The Caravan

At this moment (22 June), Bernard, Richard's chief scout, appeared, accompanied by some of his men who dressed and behaved as bedouin, with the information that a very valuable Saracen caravan was in the area bringing treasure, supplies and reinforcements to Saladin from Egypt. This was quite sufficient to spur the Crusaders into action and Richard quickly assembled a striking force. He even invited the Duke of Burgundy and his Frenchmen to join them, to which the canny duke agreed, provided that the French received one-third of the spoils (which was a somewhat greater proportion than their numbers warranted).

As will already have become clear, Richard was good in most military situations, but was at his very best where quick reaction, rapid planning and daring execution were concerned. Thus, the force, consisting of some 1,000 knights, each with a lightly armed man-at-arms sitting behind him on his horse, was quickly formed-up and briefed. Richard, planning well ahead, had also already sent some men to

Ascalon to obtain food and bring it to a rendezvous at La Galatie. The main body was on the road by mid afternoon and reached the rendezvous well after dark, having ridden the last part of the journey by the light of a splendid moon. Unfortunately for Richard, he and his army always lived in a goldfish bowl where the Saracens were concerned, and the ever present enemy scouts had seen the large and well-armed party leaving the main camp, which they reported immediately to Saladin. The Saracen general realised that the Crusaders must have learnt of the caravan and dispatched a rescue party of some 500 men. While pausing at La Galatie, Richard, who was also dressed as a bedouin, accompanied three of his local scouts forward to confirm the location of the caravan. He then returned to his troops and led them through the remainder of the night and attacked the Saracen encampment just as dawn broke.

The reinforcements dispatched by Saladin had found the convoy and warned the commander of the imminent danger – he decided that it would be unwise to attempt to move such a large number of men and animals in the dark. He was wrong and the guards ringing the convoy were taken totally by surprise when Richard and his men swept through them in the dawn attack. The convoy managed to split into three and the Crusaders captured one group complete and abandoned horses, camels and baggage from the other two. The booty which fell into Crusader hands included 4,700 camels and dromedaries, huge numbers of mules and asses, together with their loads of gold, silver, weapons, armour, tents, herbs and spices, medicines, money and clothing. The Crusaders estimated that they killed approximately 1,300 Turkish horsemen and an unquantifiable number of foot soldiers, who were trodden to death in the melee.

Back to Jerusalem

Richard and his men marched on to Bethaven, some 4 miles from Jaffa, where they divided up the spoils, and the next day they went on to Ramla, where Count Henry arrived with the men he had brought from Acre. Here Richard distributed the captured animals, although an unsought consequence was that after a few days the demand for grain drove its price so high that few could afford it. For his part, Saladin was dismayed by this major military disaster and realised that when Richard and his raiding party returned to the main body, the Crusaders would almost certainly march on Jerusalem. Accordingly, he gave orders for the water supplies around the city to be interrupted, with springs and wells blocked or poisoned, and cisterns destroyed.

Richard was perfectly correct in his belief that Saladin was in constant receipt of reports of what was going on in the Crusader camp, including at the highest levels, and it is known that such reports were detailed, very accurate and delivered within a very short time. It is not clear whether these emanated from spies or traitors, but they were so detailed that they could not have come only from scouts observing from a distance. Thus, while he was recovering from the loss of the caravan, Saladin was informed that there was yet further dissension among the Crusaders about whether or not to march on Jerusalem, the arguments centring upon the problem of water for the horses, with Richard pointing out that all the wells and cisterns around the city had been 'corrupted' (poisoned) by the Saracens so that there was no safe water source within a reasonable distance. Someone suggested a river at some distance from Jerusalem and that half the horses should be taken to the river at a time, leaving the other half with the besieging force, a suggestion which Richard found highly unsatisfactory, saying that as soon as one division had gone off with its beasts for water, the Saracen garrison would attack those that remained outside the walls and all would be lost.

By this time, feeling between the French contingent under the Duke of Burgundy and the rest of the army was running high. The French accused Richard of being half-hearted in his intention to reach the Holy City, while their pride had been hurt at having to depend upon Richard for money, although their one-third share of the spoil from the caravan had at last made them independent. For their part, the other contingents considered the French aloof and arrogant, both in their general attitude and because not only did they frequently take a view contrary to the remainder of the army, but they now also insisted on having their own separate campsite. This anti-French feeling was exacerbated when it became known that the Duke of Burgundy had composed a song that was very disparaging about Richard.

A council was once again formed and this time the arrangements were even more elaborate. It started with the selection of 300 men, who were responsible for electing twelve of their number to make a further selection. This resulted in a group of three, from whose decision no appeal would be allowed and, yet again, these final arbiters voted not to go to Jerusalem. The Crusaders were desperately disappointed as they were only about four hours' march from the Holy City, but they immediately began to pull back (5 July) and spent that night midway between St Jorge de Lidde and Ramla, moving on the next day to a camp below Casel Maen. Here the army, dispirited, worn out and bitterly disappointed, began to break up.

More Negotiations

Richard now saw no alternative but to return to negotiations with the Saracens and he sent a message to Saphadin stating that he was agreeable to a proposal for a truce made at the previous meeting at Ramla, which would enable him to return to Europe, sort out his problems and then come back to the Holy Land. Saladin, knowing that the weakness of the Crusader army gave him the upper hand, refused unless Ascalon was razed to the ground. Richard recognised this as a negotiating position and immediately established one of his own by sending 300 troops (Hospitallers, Templars and others) to flatten Darum, while others were sent to carry on the restoration work at Ascalon. This done, the army returned to Jaffa in a despondent mood, where the sick were dropped off and Richard, with the fitter members of his army, headed north to Acre. Thus, according to the chronicler: 'The army returned to Acre, broken up, with a heavy heart, for God did not as yet judge them worthy of the higher bounties of his grace.'

CHAPTER 9

The Battle of Jaffa

Having left a small garrison, plus the sick, wounded and disheartened at Jaffa, Richard and his army pressed on to Acre, the bulk on foot, with the ships keeping pace and supplying provisions at intervals. It was the reverse of the great advance from Acre to Jaffa of the previous year, but this time the Saracens did not interfere and the men were much fitter and more used to marching, so it took only five or six days, the Crusaders arriving on Sunday 26 July 1192. Once again, the king returned to his plan to hold the entire coastal strip: he had dismantled and vacated Darum, repaired and garrisoned Ascalon and already held Jaffa, Caiaphas and Acre, while King Henry and Queen Isabella held Tyre. That left Beirut as the only port in Saracen hands, so, on arriving in Acre, Richard dispatched a naval reconnaissance party northwards to assess the new target, while he prepared to follow on with his army.

Richard had, however, left a hostage to fortune – the unsupported garrison at Jaffa – which, as Saladin well knew, was composed mainly of the sick and wounded. Saladin also knew from his scouts that Richard was at Acre and considering an attack further north. These two factors, coupled with continuing intelligence reports about the poor state and internal dissensions within the Crusader army, led Saladin to seize the initiative. He quickly assembled a large force and struck swiftly and hard, arriving outside the city of Jaffa on Sunday 26 July and commencing the attack the following morning.

The Crusader garrison resisted as best it could and prevented Saladin from achieving a quick victory, with the result that on Wednesday 29 July the Saracens settled down for a full-blown siege, with four powerful *petrariae* (stone-throwers) and two mangonels being erected within a very few days. Aided by these machines, the Saracens broke through the outer walls on 31 July, forcing the defending Crusaders to withdraw into the citadel. Unfortunately for Saladin, his attack then lost much of its momentum as his troops, who had not won any victories for some time, declined to obey orders to continue the assault and instead set about some serious killing and looting in the outer city. Those Crusaders unable to get into the citadel in time headed for the harbour where they boarded ships. One of them was the garrison commander, Alberic of Rheims, and when he was recognised and accused of cowardice and dereliction of duty, he returned ashore.

The Saracen attack had been very rapid and one of those in the citadel was the newly elected Patriarch of Jerusalem, who happened to be in Jaffa at the time; after showing considerable bravery, he made an unusual proposal to Saladin. This was that there should be a temporary truce until 3 p.m. the following day (1 August) – if help had not arrived by that time the garrison would surrender, following which all would pay an agreed sum as compensation for the truce.

Saladin probably knew that the garrison had managed to dispatch a messenger to Acre just before his men had sealed off the city, but presumably he thought the garrison's request somewhat quixotic and agreed to it in the belief that not even Richard could react with the necessary force and in the time available. A number of the leading noblemen in the garrison gave themselves up as hostages to Saladin to provide surety for the deal and everyone settled down to wait.

The King Returns to Jaffa

Richard was indeed still at Acre, where he was preparing to leave for Europe. He had already sent seven galleys to assault Beirut and intended to call in there to ensure their success before continuing on his voyage to Cyprus. He was in his tent, discussing plans for the departure the following morning when the messenger arrived from Jaffa. Richard immediately determined on a rescue and all of those with him at Acre were keen to go to the aid of their fellow Crusaders, except for the French, who refused absolutely to move, saying that they would never again serve under Richard's command. The king, by now well used to Gallic intransigence, simply ignored them and dispatched a force of all available Templars, Hospitallers and other knights down the coastal route, while he put to sea in seven galleys, with a smaller force of Angevin and English knights, together with some Genoese and Pisans.

When the land force reached Caesarea it received intelligence of Saracen ambushes along the route south, which caused considerable delays, while the naval force was first becalmed and then split up by a storm. True to form, however, Richard's galley was the first on the scene at Jaffa on Saturday 1 August, accompanied by only two of the other six galleys. Ashore, the Saracens had demanded that the inhabitants of Jaffa start to leave the citadel and pay the agreed amount of money laid down in the truce, but when the first to leave the gates paid up they were immediately beheaded. It is scarcely surprising that this caused consternation among those following – they promptly closed the gate and appealed to God to deliver them from certain death.

Such help was indeed close at hand, as Richard's ship was approaching the shore (it was about 9 a.m. on 1 August), but all that could be seen from the galley was a shore lined with Saracens firing arrows. It appeared at first that the rescuers were too late and Richard had just called his ships together to confer on what to do next, when a priest leapt from the battlements into the sea and swam out to Richard's ship, where he told the king that there was still some hope and that some fifty knights were holding out in the citadel. Telling his comrades that 'a curse [will] light on him who hesitates', Richard ordered the galleys to pull for the shore and as soon as they were in the shallows he leapt into the water, which came up to his waist, a sword in one hand and an arbalest in the other. The king, followed by eighty knights, a few foot soldiers, and even some of the ship's crew excited by the prospect of battle and of rescuing fellow Crusaders, managed not only to obtain a foothold on the beach, but actually to clear it.

Saladin already knew that a Crusader rescue force was on its way but appears to have been confident of concluding the affair before his opponents' arrival, so he was as surprised as his troops when Richard's red galley appeared off the city. As soon as he heard the news, Saladin ordered an immediate assault on the citadel where the remaining Crusaders had little choice but to agree to surrender, although they used every possible delaying tactic to give their rescuers time to reach them. Richard's arrival was quickly known to the Saracens, since the King of England, taking his motif from his flaming red hair, wore a red tunic, bore a red heraldic device on his shield and even his galley was painted red – it was, therefore, difficult not to know of his presence on the battlefield.

As in any amphibious landing throughout the ages, the Crusaders were extraordinarily vulnerable as they crossed the gap between their ships and the high water mark, and it is surprising that the Saracens facing them do not appear to have offered any serious resistance. This may have been because Saladin and most of his commanders and troops were out of sight supervising the surrender of the Crusaders in the citadel; indeed, the Patriarch of Jerusalem was already in Saladin's tent. A second reason for the lack of serious resistance on the beach may have been that the Saracen troops, whose morale was not as high as usual during this whole operation, recognised the dreaded and ferocious King of England and there was probably a general reluctance to be in the front line against such a noted warrior.

As soon as they were reasonably secure ashore, Richard ordered his men to grab whatever wood and rubbish they could to erect a palisade. This provided them with a temporary base and leaving a few to hold it, Richard led the rush into the town, where they found large numbers of Saracens occupied in looting. The king quickly had his banner hoisted on the ramparts which encouraged those in the citadel to emerge and join in the fighting, catching the Saracens between two forces. Such was the ferocity of the attack and so quickly did the news of Richard's arrival spread that the Saracen soldiers, even though they greatly outnumbered the Crusaders, withdrew from the city in confusion to the village of Yazur, which was a safe distance away, leaving their leaders with little option but to fall back with them.

It took Saladin some time to bring his army under control, but as soon as he had done so he sent emissaries to visit Richard to see whether an agreement might be negotiated. Richard and Saladin each had their own reasons to need a temporary peace but the negotiations stalled, once again, over the future of the fortified port of Ascalon. Richard wanted the port because it would give the Crusaders control of the entire coast and enable them to threaten Egypt, while Saladin needed to prevent the Crusaders from exercising such control. Richard wanted a truce, because his horses were stiff, exhausted and dizzy after standing in ships for a month or more, and would not be fully fit for several days.

Saladin's Counter-Attack

With the negotiations at a stalemate, Richard joined his men and all spent the next three days in repairing the fortifications. He was the King of England and the mightiest warrior in Christendom, but was never too grand to join his men in hard physical labour when the occasion required it, and his men, from the highest to the lowest, loved him for it. Dusk on Tuesday 4 August found Richard, Count Henry and nine other knights still hard at work outside the city wall, and together with some foot soldiers they made camp where they were, which, as it happened, was the spot where Saladin had pitched his tents only a few days earlier.

The Saracens were, however, smarting after their recent defeat and had been keeping their greatest enemy under close observation. Thus, Saladin hatched a plan for a two-pronged attack; one party was to conduct a noisy diversionary attack on the city defences, while the other party was to attempt the much more important task of 'snatching' King Richard from his vulnerable campsite.

The Saracen operation took place on the night of Tuesday/Wednesday 4/5 August 1192, with the 'snatch squad' consisting of two groups, with Saladin present and among the leading elements, so that he was actually able to see King Richard's tents. However, it appears that the two elements proceeded to fall out with each other over which of them should attack on foot and which on horseback, causing a serious delay, as a result of which they did not approach Richard's camp until dawn was breaking. Fortunately for the Crusaders, a Genoese mercenary spotted them. According to Ambroise this soldier walked out from the position as the result of God inclining his mind 'to go forth into the neighbouring plains at dawn,' although any experienced soldier reading that line will know immediately that such early morning individual forays are not so much to fulfil the need to communicate with the Almighty as to answer the more prosaic call of nature. But, whatever the reason, the Genoese soldier heard the noise of the approaching raiding party and rushed back to the campsite, shouting 'To arms! To arms!'

Richard and his comrades just had time to don their mail vests over their nightshirts and then stood in a small circle, snarling, according to a Saracen chronicler, 'like the dogs of war', clearly prepared to fight to the death. Saladin tried desperately to persuade his men to attack, but none of them was prepared to make the first move and Saladin, appreciating that a continuation of the stand-off would only result in a major loss of face, called the operation off.

Meanwhile, the other element of the Saracen attack had already managed to penetrate into the city, and the fighting soon became general, with Richard, still outside the city walls, in the thick of it. Richard was always a good military leader, but particularly so in emergencies, where his quick mind and superb tactical sense enabled him to devise rapid and effective plans. In this case, he and his men established a palisade from bits and pieces of wood lying around, which gave them a temporary base with a degree of security, and thus a brief breathing space. The next step was to assemble a counter-attack force of sixty knights – of which only six had horses – and then, leaving one group on the palisade, he led his men into the city, where they managed to eject the astonished Saracens.

The Battle Continues

Realising that the battle was by no means over and that the Saracens, who had a seemingly overwhelming superiority of numbers, would soon return to the attack, Richard quickly organised his troops for another defensive action. His chosen battlesite was a piece of flat ground outside the city walls where he had just built the temporary palisade. Richard deployed his few knights nearest the sea with the Church of St Nicholas on their left and since this seemed to be the area of greatest threat he positioned himself there also. On the right were Pisans and Genoese, with other troops intermingled among them.

Richard's plan, devised on the spot and under threat of imminent attack, was simple but devastating, and was based on his infantry, who were deployed in three ranks. The front rank was composed of pikemen, each man with his right knee on the ground, his left leg bent and his shield or buckler in his left hand. In his right hand he held his pike at 45 degrees, the base stuck firmly in the sand and the pointed iron head at exactly the level of a horses's chest or belly. These men knelt thigh to thigh, thus giving each other confidence as well as stabilising the formation. The second rank was composed of crossbowmen, firing through the gaps between the pikemen (and protected by the latters' shields), while the third rank consisted of men whose task was to reload the crossbows and pass them forward to the second rank as required. The result was a veritable hedgehog, with the crossbowmen keeping up a constant, aimed fire, while the pikes presented a virtually impenetrable obstacle to any Saracen venturing close enough. Finally, the handful of mounted knights were held as a reserve under Richard's personal command, whose task was to charge any small group of Saracens foolish enough to provide a worthwhile target.

It is sometimes alleged that Richard promised personally to behead anyone who fell out of the line, but there is no evidence of this in the reports from those present at the battle. Indeed, his speech was quite different in tone:

> Courage, my brave men and let not the attack of the enemy disturb you.
> Bear up against the frowns of fortune, and you will rise above them.
> Every thing may be borne by brave men; adversity sheds a light upon the

virtues of mankind, as certainly as prosperity casts over them a shade; there is no room for flight, and to attempt to flee is to provoke certain death. Be brave, therefore, and let the urgency of the case sharpen your valour: brave men should either conquer nobly, or gloriously die. Martyrdom is a boon which we should receive with willing mind: but before we die, let us whilst still alive do what may avenge our deaths, giving thanks to God that it has been our lot to die martyrs. This will be the end of our labours, the termination of our life, and of our battles.

This is far from being a threat that Richard would behead any who ran, but simply pointing out, quite correctly, that if the line broke, for whatever reason, then all would be killed by the Saracens.

As soon as Richard had delivered this exhortation the first attack came in. According to one observer the first charge comprised seven groups of a thousand men each, which is almost certainly a gross overestimate – the actual numbers do not really matter, since it is clear that a large cavalry force, greatly outnumbering the Crusaders, was involved. As the Saracen cavalry neared this defensive 'hedgehog' they realised the danger into which they were charging and turned away at the last minute, thus not only failing to break the Crusader line but offering ideal targets to the crossbowmen as they turned. Several successive waves tried the same tactic, but the Crusader infantry stood absolutely firm, their position being enhanced by the growing numbers of dead Saracens and horses a short distance in front of their position. Once again, this presaged a later event when, in the late afternoon of 18 June 1815 during the Battle of Waterloo, the British infantry squares stood firm against the repeated charges of the French cavalry.

After one particular Saracen charge, Richard chose his moment and led the Crusader cavalry in a charge from the left flank, riding straight into the Saracen horsemen as they were in the middle of their turn away. The Crusader momentum was so great that they actually emerged on the far side of the Saracen line. The fight between the Crusader knights and the Saracen cavalry proved very bloody, with the latter striving to get at the king, whose death or capture would not only have been a great triumph for whoever was responsible, but would also have almost certainly brought about a Crusader defeat. Richard seemed to be everywhere at once: he saved the Earl of Leicester who had been unhorsed, and then rescued Ralph de Mauleon, who had been captured and was being led away a prisoner. He slew many of the enemy, his sword: 'shone like lightning; some of them were cloven in two from their helmet to their teeth, whilst others lost their heads, arms, and other members, which were lopped off at a single blow.'

At one point the battle seemed lost and the sailors withdrew into their galleys, while some Saracens managed to get back into the town. Richard, on hearing of this, took two knights and two crossbowmen and rushed into the town where he encountered the Saracens and slew them all, capturing two of their horses in the process; at this, the other Saracens within the walls made good their escape before meeting the dreaded King of England. Having secured the town, Richard went down to the shore where he found that the sailors had been joined by a number of soldiers, and he quickly persuaded them to return to the fray, leaving just five men on board each galley as guards. Richard led the men in person back to the scene of the fighting and then threw himself into the thick of the fray, where the enemy tried to first isolate him from other Crusaders and then either kill or capture him. They succeeded in the first, but conspicuously failed in the second, as Richard laid about them, dealing death and destruction to many, before making his way back to the Crusader lines.

Crusader Victory

The battle had started at dawn on 5 August and it was almost sunset before the fighting at last died down. Contemporary reports suggest that the Saracens lost about 700 men and 1,500 horses, while the Crusaders claim to have lost only a very few killed, although large numbers were wounded. The pace had been intense, the fighting furious, and on the Crusader side both the cavalry and infantry had behaved supremely well. The retreat of some men to the galleys need not be given great emphasis; such things happen in many battles and Richard resolved it calmly and confidently, personally leading the men back to their duty, which was just the example they needed.

This was a clear Crusader victory, in which Richard played an absolutely crucial role, as a commander, as a leader and as a warrior. Perhaps the most noteworthy feature of the battle is the final phase in which the infantry – so skilfully deployed by Richard – were a key ingredient in the successful outcome. Indeed, they were one of the earliest examples of that 'thin red line' with which English infantry has time and again provided a stubborn and triumphant defence against cavalry – this Crusader example was later followed at Crecy, Poitiers, Agincourt, Blenheim, Minden and Waterloo.

The pace of events in this most memorable of battles is breathtaking, as Richard repeatedly just managed to stave off defeat. His personal contribution was exceptional: he was always at the point of greatest threat, always in the thick of the fighting, and always in imminent danger of being either killed or captured, but managing to escape by the skin of his teeth. Richard was not just a 'mighty warrior' however, as the Battle of Jaffa clearly showed that he also had a brilliant grasp of tactics and repeatedly deployed his very limited resources to maximum effect.

It appears at first sight that Saladin and the Saracens had not done particularly well. However, the Saracen army was simply exhausted, the great majority of men having been fighting and marching continuously for several years. Like Richard's, Saladin's army was made up of various contingents with varying degrees of autonomy and the commander had to cajole them as much as command them. Moreover, despite the excellence of their own commander, many individual Saracens appear to have become overawed, not only by Richard's reputation, but by his actual performance.

CHAPTER 10

The End of the Campaign

With the fighting having ended at Jaffa on 5 August, emissaries were once again sent between the armies, the first from Saladin telling Richard that the Saracen leader intended to come and seize the king, if only he could be sure that the king would remain long enough. To this the king replied that he would most assuredly await the Sultan's arrival, and would be very willing to defend himself, provided that he had the strength to stand upright.

Now that the excitement of the battle was over, however, Richard found himself in a dangerously exposed position. His army was small and Saladin's much larger army dominated the countryside outside the immediate confines of Jaffa. Richard knew that the French had moved from Acre down to Caesarea, so he dispatched Count Henry with a request that they would come to his assistance, but this the French totally refused to do, despite the danger of their fellow Crusaders' situation. Meanwhile, he was also negotiating with Saladin, but the same sticking point remained – Ascalon. Saladin still demanded control of the fortress and Richard persisted in refusing to hand it over.

By this time, Richard was in a bad state. He was physically and mentally exhausted from the strains of the campaign, having had virtually no rest since landing at Acre so many months before and this, combined with the stench of rotting corpses in the streets of Jaffa forced him to take to his sick-bed. He was also extremely concerned about events at home; indeed, had it not been for Saladin's attack, he would have been well on the way to England by now. The only thing that cheered him at this point was the news that the Duke of Burgundy, who had borrowed such huge sums of money and yet had proved such a thorn in his side, was gravely ill at Acre. This news was followed some days later by the announcement that the duke had died on 25 August, an event which caused Richard no little pleasure and seems to have speeded his recovery. He decided, as a first step, that he should go to Acre, where the better facilities, more pleasant atmosphere and the presence of his wife Berengaria and sister Joan, would help him to recover his strength.

Accordingly, Richard sent for Count Henry and the leaders of the Templars and Hospitallers to inform them of this, and to give them instructions for the garrisoning and defence of Ascalon and Jaffa. To Richard's consternation, however, his listeners were united in their refusal to countenance such a course, telling him that without his presence these places would be impossible to defend. Not surprisingly, Richard considered this both unfeeling and unhelpful. His first reaction was to issue a proclamation that whoever wanted to receive the king's pay should assemble to receive it; some 50 knights and 2,000 infantry responded, although it is not clear how he intended to employ them.

All this was to no avail, however, as his health worsened and having decided that there was no alternative, he sent for Saphadin, Saladin's brother, and told him that he was ready to discuss a truce. When told of this, Saladin was by no means unwilling and an agreement was quickly hammered out and signed on 2 September 1192, the main terms being:

❖ Ascalon would be destroyed and not rebuilt for three years from the following Easter (i.e. 28 March 1193).

❖ The Crusaders would be allowed to occupy Jaffa and the surrounding area without let or hindrance.

❖ Both sides would be free to travel wherever they wished and there would be no fighting.

❖ Christian pilgrims would have free access to the Holy Sepulchre, and would be allowed to trade throughout the whole area.

Richard was criticised for agreeing to what were regarded as unfavourable terms, particularly by the French, but the facts were inescapable. First, he had a small army and Saladin's much larger army was only two miles away. Second, other Crusaders, especially the French, had refused to come to his aid. Third, there seemed to be no satisfactory end to the campaign under the current conditions and the three-year truce would give the Crusaders an opportunity to resolve and improve matters. Finally, Richard simply could not continue to ignore the events in his kingdom of England and his various territories in France, which demanded his presence if disaster was to be avoided.

When everything had been settled there occurred an exchange of messages probably unique in military history between two commanders-in-chief. It started with Richard, who sent ambassadors to Saladin with a personal message. This was delivered to Saladin in the presence of many of his subordinate commanders and informed the Saracen leader that Richard:

> . . . had only asked for a truce of three years for the purpose of revisiting his country, and collecting more men and money, wherewith to return and rescue all the land of Jerusalem from his domination – if, indeed, Saladin should have the courage to face him in the field.

Saladin immediately replied that:

> He entertained such an exalted opinion of King Richard's honour, mag-
> nanimity, and general excellence, that he would rather lose his
> dominions to him than to any other king that he had ever seen – always
> supposing that he was obliged to lose his dominions at all.

It is impossible to consider this exchange without being impressed by
the nobility of the language, the obvious respect each had for the other and
the gentle humour – teasing, almost – in the final part of each message.
Both of them were commanders of great skill and warriors of proven
courage; this exchange also showed that they were great gentlemen as well,
and it can only be a matter for regret that they never actually met.

The truce having been signed, Richard left Jaffa and headed north to
Caiaphas, which had recently been vacated by the French, who had
returned to Acre to prepare for their own return home. However, despite
their vitriolic criticism of Richard for signing the truce, the French now
decided that they wished to take advantage of its terms and visit
Jerusalem. On hearing of this, Richard finally lost patience and sent a
message to Saladin and Saphadin that they should only allow people to
visit the Holy Sepulchre who had a passport signed by either himself or
Count Henry. At this, most of the French gave up and left for home.
Whereupon Richard announced that anyone who wished to go to
Jerusalem might now do so and many Crusaders visited the city in three
large groups, being given a totally secure and by no means unfriendly
passage by the Saracens.

The third of these large parties was led by the Bishop of Salisbury,
who was summoned to meet the great Saladin and the two men had a
long and cordial discussion. Part of this concerned King Richard, and
having listened to the bishop's views, Saladin then gave his opinion of his
opponent:

I have long been aware that your king is a man of the greatest honour and bravery, but he is imprudent, not to say foolishly so, in thrusting himself so frequently into great danger, and shows too great reckless-ness of his own life. For my own part, of however large territories I might be the king, I would rather have abundance of wealth, with wisdom and moderation, than display immoderate valour and rashness.

Richard was at Acre preparing to leave, but before embarking he had two matters to settle. The first concerned William de Pratelles, who had voluntarily surrendered himself to the Saracens in a skirmish, claiming to be Richard, thus saving his king from the humiliation of capture, and Richard now exchanged ten high-ranking Saracen prisoners in order to obtain this brave knight's release. Secondly, the king called on anyone claiming to be owed money by him to come forward, and all were repaid.

All was now completed and the king sailed away on Friday 9 October 1192, never to return. If the memory of their adventures in the Holy Land remained long in the minds of the Crusaders, so too did the name of the King of England remain vivid in the Holy Land for centuries to come, where he:

... was so dreaded that the fear of him was in the heart and mouths of the Saracens. Insomuch that when their children wept they would say to them 'Be quiet – the king of England is coming!' And if their horses started they would jestingly say 'Is the king of England in front of us then?'

CHAPTER 11

Main Fleet to the Holy Land

Where King Richard was concerned, the Third Crusade was a combined land/sea undertaking from start to finish. However, as all the ships involved were essentially chartered transports with civilian crews, rather than government-owned warships, the relevance of the maritime contribution has frequently been overlooked. In reality, this was England's first great maritime adventure, in which Richard employed large numbers of ships to conduct the strategic deployment of his army from England to the Holy Land, thus totally eliminating the overland march through eastern Europe to Byzantium and thence across Asia Minor and south through Syria, which had proved so costly to the First and Second Crusades.

Furthermore, his ships enabled him to make tactical attacks on enemy shipping off the coast of the Holy Land, conduct assault landings on enemy-held beaches, and, in addition, provide the logistical support for the army, without which land operations would have been impossible. The full story of each of these operations is described elsewhere in this book – this chapter brings together the maritime aspects of the Third Crusade.

Types of Vessel

Various types of vessel were in use at the end of the twelfth century, and identifying the different categories from contemporary accounts is difficult, not least because it would appear that the northern European and Mediterranean sailors sometimes had different names for the same type. Furthermore, all the chroniclers were landsmen, whose understanding of maritime matters was less than complete.

The largest and fastest ship was the *dromon*, which had one, two, or in the case of the ship sunk by Richard off Beirut, three masts, each carrying a large lateen sail, and with up to one hundred oars. The *buss*, also known as the *tarida*, had thirty oars plus a single mast and a square sail, one of which was described as carrying forty warhorses, forty knights and forty foot soldiers, plus all their equipment, with a crew of fifteen. Contemporaries described the busses as capable of carrying a full year's supply of food for all their passengers, crew and horses, although this seems somewhat over optimistic, both in terms of the sheer quantity involved and the very limited ability to preserve foodstuffs. In any event, no sea voyage of the period ever lasted that long.

When Richard left Marseilles his fleet included fourteen busses, which were described as 'vessels of vast size, wonderful speed, and great strength'. The flagship had 'three rudders, thirteen anchors, thirty oars, two sails, and triple oars of every kind: moreover it had everything that a ship can want in pairs – saving only the mast and boat.' The organisation of this squadron was such that there was 'one very skillful captain and fourteen chosen mariners were under his orders'; i.e. the captain was responsible for the entire squadron, with one of the 'chosen mariners' in command of each vessel (including the captain's own).

A specific vessel known to have been with the English fleet on the Third Crusade was the *Esnecca Regis*, belonging to Richard. An *esnecca* was a long, narrow, clinker-built boat with oars for entering and leaving harbour, and a single mast supporting a single square sail, which was used in the open sea. The *esnecca* had no deck, but the bow and stern may have been covered to provide some sort of shelter. The design was directly descended from that of the Viking longship and its name, which means 'snake', may have been descriptive of its low-lying appearance with its prominent forecastle resembling that of a swimming sea-serpent. This particular vessel of Richard's was the last known example in English service, being normally used to conduct the king to and fro across the English Channel; it was captained by Alan Trenchemer (whose surname means to 'cleave through the waves') and had a crew of sixty.

Planning

The voyage to the Holy Land was clearly planned very carefully. There had been previous English overseas naval operations, but nothing on the scale that Richard now intended. A squadron of thirty ships, commanded by Edgar Æthling, took part in the First Crusade, where, quite by chance, they arrived off Antioch at a critical juncture in the siege (October 1097 – June 1098) and were able to capture the fortress of Laodicea, thus saving the Crusaders from starvation. Some fifty years later a fleet of 170 ships sailed from Dartmouth to Lisbon in 1147 to help King Alfonso I of Portugal in his fight against the Moors.

What Richard now planned, however, was on a scale and of a complexity that completely overshadowed all previous undertakings. The overall intention was that the king and one group would travel overland to Marseille, where they would meet the fleet which had started from various ports in England and Richard's French territories, and then sailed around the Iberian peninsula. Having met at Marseille the combined group would then sail to Sicily, where they would spend the winter and, as soon as the sailing season opened, carry on to the Holy Land. The chartering of ships for this great enterprise started in June 1189, and assembling the fleet took time, but was very carefully organised. The full records have not survived, but it is known that the contribution of England's south-eastern ports was forty-five vessels. Of these, thirty-three came from the Cinque Ports, three each from Shoreham and Southampton, another four from three named individuals, one which Richard provided to the Hospitallers and, finally, Richard's own *Esnecca Regis*. The English fleet which sailed to the Mediterranean is known to have numbered well over one hundred vessels, so the others would have come from the Thames, from south-western ports such as Brixham, Dartmouth and Plymouth, from Bristol, and the remainder from Richard's French possessions.

Command

Richard's preparations for his fleet were thorough, with five men appointed to the principal commands: Girard, Archbishop of Auch; Bernard, Bishop of Bayonne; Robert de Sablun; Richard de Camville; and William de Forz of Oléron. Richard also issued one of the earliest known naval disciplinary codes, which seems draconian and was doubtless intended to be so. The punishment for killing a man was to be tied to the corpse and then, depending upon where the offence took place, either being thrown into the sea or buried in a common grave. Drawing or using a knife with intent to wound resulted in the offending fist being cut off, while striking a blow warranted being dipped in the sea three times. Theft, always considered serious, especially if from a comrade, was punished by being shorn, tarred and feathered, and then abandoned ashore at the next landfall.[13]

The 'Sailing Season'

Medieval vessels were not particularly seaworthy and the winter months were considered unsuitable for voyages, particularly for galleys. In the fourth century AD, the Roman Vegetius was very specific where the Mediterranean was concerned, stating that oared galleys must not sail between 14 September and 26 May annually, while sailing ships had a shorter closed season stretching from 10 November to 10 March. By the twelfth century these were not so rigidly laid down, but even the vessels of that time could not cope with the strong northerly gales and short, breaking seas – these were more than enough to keep fleets in harbour over the winter months.

Voyage to Outremer

The fleet loaded in the early spring of 1190 and sailed in small groups the first leaving immediately after Easter which fell on 25 March and was the earliest practicable date after the inclement winter months. One such group consisting of thirty-seven vessels assembled at Dartmouth in Devon and sailed in early April; by 3 May it was off the Spanish coast when, like all the other groups, it was hit by a major storm. The vessels were dispersed and at least four were lost, the survivors limping into various Portuguese ports to recover and to repair the damage. Another group, comprising sixty-three vessels, followed by a smaller group of nine, sailed into Lisbon, where its crews' behaviour was such that no less than 700 men were arrested in one night, earning the English sailors a somewhat unsavoury reputation.

These seventy-two vessels sailed again on 24 July, joined up with another group of thirty-four ships waiting at the mouth of the Tagus, and passed safely through the Straits of Gibraltar on 1 August, reaching

Marseille on 22 August, some five months after leaving England. Due to the storm and other delays, the fleet had missed Richard who had arrived at Marseille at the beginning of August and (as usual) lacking the patience to wait, he had then chartered a number of local galleys and departed on 7 August. So, after a stay of eight days, the main fleet sailed again, reaching Messina on 14 September 1190.

Richard and his group at Marseille split into two for their onward journey. One party, led by Baldwin, Archbishop of Canterbury, Hubert, Bishop of Salisbury and Ranulf de Glanville, sailed direct to the Holy Land, leaving Marseille on about 7 August and arriving at Tyre on 16 September 1190. It seems to have been a quick and uneventful voyage, although they had to spend some three weeks in Tyre recovering from various forms of sickness, before sailing south to reach Acre on 12 October, where they were able to inform the garrison that the King of

Table I: Third Crusade: English Fleet Outward Voyage

Leg	Dates From	To	Days at sea	Place From	To	Distance (miles)[1]
1	26 March 1190	12 May 1190[2]	48	Dartmouth[3]	Lisbon	1,000
2	24 July 1190	22 August 1190	29	Lisbon	Marseille	1,400
3	30 August 1190	14 September 1190	15	Marseille	Messina	900
4	10 April 1191	6 May 1191	26	Messina	Cyprus	1,300
5	25 May 1191	2 June 1191	7	Cyprus	Acre	400
		TOTAL	125		TOTAL	5,000

1 Approximate distances; due to tacking and adverse winds, actual distances covered would have been much greater.

2 Actual date of arrival is not recorded but was sometime during the second week of May.

3 The sailing dates for the other groups sailing from different ports will have varied by a week or two.

England was on his way. Richard and the remainder of his men travelled by sea and land down the coast of Italy arriving in Messina on 23 September. They then spent the winter in Sicily, from whence they departed on the final leg of their voyage to the Holy Land on 10 April 1191.

Various historians have commented on the apparently excessive length of Richard's stay in Sicily. However, he arrived on the island on 23 September 1190, which was at the very end of the 'sailing season' and when his great fleet sailed from Messina on 10 April 1191, it was just five days before Easter (which fell on 14 April that year) and was probably the first prudent opportunity for such a long voyage. Even then, it was a compromise between the requirements of the galleys and the sailing ships, and, as events were to show, the fleet had probably left too early.

The intention was to head directly for the Holy Land, but in an age when open ocean voyages were avoided as much as possible, this involved calling at a succession of islands on the way. The fleet now numbered 216 ships, comprising the survivors of the main fleet that had sailed from England and France between March and April 1190, those chartered by Richard since arriving in the Mediterranean, and a number presented to Richard by King Tancred of Sicily.

This fleet, which was large by any standard, comprised thirteen dromons, fifty-three galleys and 150 busses and was deployed in eight lines. The leading line consisted of three dromons, one of which was commanded by Stephen of Turnham and carried Richard's sister, Queen Joanna of Sicily, and fiancée, Princess Berengaria of Navarre, while the other two carried the main part of Richard's weapons and some of the treasury. The remaining lines consisted of thirteen, fourteen, twenty, thirty, forty and sixty vessels respectively, with the eighth line consisting of some thirty-six galleys, including Richard's own ship. One reason for this large and cumbersome formation was mutual defence against pirates, of which there were many in the Mediterranean, and the positioning of the fast galleys in the rear, coupled with Richard's well-known penchant for placing himself in the spot of greatest danger, indicates that the major threat was expected from astern. The king's treasure and the major weapons were divided among various ships and busses, so not all would be lost in event of battle or disaster.

Another reason for sailing in such a large group was that at that time open ocean voyages were rare, with vessels normally making short hops along the coast and dropping anchor on most nights. The average captain's navigational skills were poor, perhaps even non-existent in many cases, and the large convoy enabled the few skilled navigators to guide the remainder. Communications were by means of voice between adjacent ships and by trumpet between lines, with Richard, as usual, acting as the roving commander, chivvying laggards, restoring lost formations, and carrying a large lantern at the masthead to serve as a guide at night.

The fleet was becalmed the day following its departure from Messina and anchored off Mount Etna for the night. The next day, which happened to be Good Friday, brought a breeze which enabled them to make some progress, but this then freshened into a south-westerly gale, scattering the fleet and frightening almost everybody except for Richard, who remained cool and collected, directing the reassembly of the fleet the following morning. He led what ships he could find to Crete where they anchored on 17 April and it was discovered that some twenty-five vessels were missing, including that carrying Richard's sister and fiancée. After just one day, the fleet sailed on to Rhodes, arriving on the 22nd, where Richard was taken ill and went ashore to recover, while galleys were dispatched to search for the missing ships, although none were found.

Having recovered, Richard sailed again and arrived off Limassol in Cyprus on 6 May, to discover that the three dromons from the first line of the convoy had been blown to Cyprus in the storm. Two had foundered on the rocks, but the one carrying Queen Joanna and Princess Berengaria had avoided any calamity and was lying at anchor off Limassol. Most of the subsequent events in the brief campaign in Cyprus took place on land, but Richard also employed two groups of ships that were sent in opposite directions around the island, carrying troops to attack any suitable targets. This was yet another example of Richard's use of combined land/sea operations, and one which helped to drive Isaac Comnenus to a quick defeat.

Following Richard's lightning conquest of Cyprus, the main fleet sailed on 25 May and arrived at Acre on 1 June, while Richard remained in Cyprus for a few days to set up the administration of his newly acquired island. He sailed on 5 June, his fleet reinforced by a number of excellent galleys which had been captured in Cyprus; he landed at Acre on 12 June, although some of the larger transports carrying the siege train arrived a few days later.

Horse Transports

Most of the transport vessels carried horses as well as human passengers and it is known that there were three types in the Mediterranean at this time. One had a door in the ship's side and was designed to enter a harbour and load or unload its horses onto a jetty; this type did not need oars and could carry more horses. The second type had a stern ramp, so that the ship could back onto a beach, whereupon the door was opened, the ramp lowered, and the horses led or ridden directly ashore. Such a manouevre was only possible with oars, and the necessary space for oars and oarsmen reduced the number of horses that could be carried, but such a craft is a clear antecedent of the tank-landing ships of the Second World War. The third type of vessel loaded its horses alongside a jetty, but offloaded them using a crane. On some occasions where there were no harbour facilities and beaching was impossible, the vessel would heave-to offshore and use its crane to lift the horses into the sea, whereupon they would swim ashore.

Inside all types of ship the horses were secured by means of slings passing under their bellies, which meant that they could not lie down for the duration of the voyage. Several chroniclers record that, immediately after disembarking, horses had to be walked up and down for a period because they were stiff, benumbed and dizzy after standing for a month or more, and were not fully fit for several days.

A Sea Battle

There are several reports of sea fights during the Third Crusade, but the most spectacular example occurred during Richard's short voyage from Cyprus to Acre, when his galleys were heading south past Beirut, where they overhauled a very large three-masted dromon, whose size and height took them all by surprise. The Crusaders were uncertain at first of her identity, their confusion being compounded when their challenges were answered by claims, first, that the vessel was French and then that she was Genoese. Then a sailor claimed to recognise her as a Saracen vessel, which was confirmed when an English ship approached too close and was met by a hail of arrows and by Greek fire. She was on her way to Acre and was carrying 1,000 men, of whom 650 were reinforcements for the beleaguered garrison, as well as food, equipment, pots of Greek fire and 'two hundred most deadly serpents, destined to work havoc among the Christians'. Her captain, one Yakub of Aleppo, had a strong and powerful ship, with a determined crew, but he was faced by forty of Richard's galleys.

On the other side, Richard was not deterred by the small size of his ships compared to that of his adversary, and set a precedent, followed by the Royal Navy to this day, by ordering that the first duty of any captain was to lay his ship alongside the enemy's. The Crusaders tried hard to board the dromon, but the height of the vessel's deck, the oars jutting from her sides, the strength of her crew, and the volume of arrows and darts all combined to prevent them from doing so.

Richard then harangued his men and issued his usual threats of hanging and torture in the event of failure,[14] whereupon one of his galleys approached the dromon from its most vulnerable point, dead astern, and a group of men dived overboard to secure the enemy ship's rudder with ropes, forcing it to go round in a circle. There appears to have been a brief period of confusion aboard the Saracen ship, which enabled the English galleys to seize the opportunity to come alongside, allowing boarders to clamber up the ship's sides. There was then a furious hand-to-hand battle on the ship's upper deck – at one point the Saracens were pressed back into the bows – but the sudden arrival of a new group from below resulted in the Englishmen being driven back and eventually forced to return aboard their own ships.

There are two versions of what happened next. According to the Crusaders, Richard ordered his galleys haul off and form a line, where-upon they attacked as one, their oarsmen working hard to ensure that they hit the enemy with their iron-clad beaks at maximum speed. The enemy ship was holed in many places and soon sank, only some thirty-five survivors being rescued by the English. According to the Saracen version, the galley's crew, realising that defeat was inevitable, bored and hacked holes in their ship's bottom and scuttled her, with only one survivor being picked up by the English. Whichever was correct, the result was the same – the Saracen ship sank with very heavy loss of life. There can be no doubt that Captain Yakub and his men put up a very worthy resistance but, like Captain Langsdorff and the German armoured cruiser, *Graf Spee*, in December 1939, they were overwhelmed by smaller, less powerful ships acting in concert.

Tactical Operations

Richard did not employ his fleet solely as strategic transports – they were also used as tactical transports during the marches along the coast, and, in particular, when the army marched from Acre to Jaffa during August–September 1191. The ships kept pace with the army as it marched and resupplied the men at regular intervals, thus greatly reducing the amount of supplies which had to be carried by the land force, and also doing away with the need for a large supply train of pack-horses, wagons and porters.

Ships were not only used for logistic support – on at least two occasions Richard used them to conduct opposed landings. The first was the initial landing in Cyprus and the second was at Jaffa in 1192. On both these occasions, Richard and his men stormed ashore and pushed the defenders off the beach, which seems somewhat surprising since such attackers are at their most vulnerable when in the open on the beach.

A Major Achievement

It would appear that prior to his departure on the Third Crusade, Richard's nautical experience was confined to trips across the English Channel, but despite this, he showed a great understanding of naval matters. It seems clear that he must have had at least one naval adviser, who helped to plan the voyages, and in particular, the long voyage from England to the Holy Land, but the names of those involved have been lost. One of Richard's most impressive achievements is the way in which he treated his naval forces and his army as mutually supporting and, in a very modern sense, part of an integrated whole. The scope of the planning is also impressive, ranging from assembling goods and loading them onto ships, to a disciplinary code for the crews.

What is truly astonishing is that so very little went wrong. It may be a perverse way to view such affairs, but the fact is that in a series of very complex naval operations, involving many hundreds of vessels and thousands of men, covering vast distances and a period of some two years, there was not a single major disaster.

CHAPTER 12

Logistics

When reviewing military operations, logistics (the art of supply) is generally ignored, and rarely reported upon as a subject in its own right. The Third Crusade is no exception and none of the surviving accounts deals with logistics as a separate subject, although a detailed analysis shows that it was a constant problem. Logistics were, in fact, one of the deciding issues of the campaign and Richard clearly took the subject extremely seriously, both when planning the Crusade and while carrying it out. A prime example of his approach was the advice he gave to the council of leaders when they were considering the second advance on Jerusalem, telling them that:

> We are far off from the coast, and if Saladin should come down into the plain of Ramla with his host and *cut off our provisions* by guarding the ways, would not this, I ask you, be our utter ruin? Then, however, it would be too late for repentance. Besides, the circuit [i.e. circumference] of Jerusalem, so far as we hear, is very large and if our little host were to attempt to close it on every side, our numbers would not suffice for the siege and *the protection of those who bring up our stores* [my italics].

The absence of detailed contemporary statistics makes it difficult to establish the size of the problem with any precision, but with the aid of some assumptions and using one known operation, it is feasible to establish the *scale* of what was involved and to demonstrate how Richard endeavoured to overcome it. The purpose of what follows, therefore, is to describe the situation in general and then to deduce the logistical support required on the march from Acre to Jaffa, which lasted from 22 August to 10 September 1191.

As a student of Vegetius, Richard would have been familiar with the Roman's instructions that:

> The main and principal point in war is to secure plenty of provisions and to destroy the enemy by famine. An exact calculation must therefore be made before the commencement of the war as to the number of troops and the expenses incident thereto, so that the provinces may in plenty of time furnish the forage, corn, and all other kinds of provisions demanded of them to be transported.

Further:

> The ancients distributed the provisions at a fixed allowance to each man without distinction of rank ... the troops should never want for wood and forage in winter or water in summer.

Preparing for the Campaign

It is quite clear that Richard started making plans even before his father's death, since as soon as he became king, he began issuing instructions. His first priority was to set about obtaining money, using both traditional methods of taxation, as well as novel methods which at the time verged on extortion. This money was then used to purchase equipment and supplies for the Crusade. Actual quantities are seldom recorded in the accounts that remain, but it is known that the warlike supplies assembled in England included crossbows and bolts, bows and arrows and hauberks, as well as stakes and beams for siege engines. One particular item where quantities are mentioned is horseshoes, surviving records showing that 50,000 were provided by the county of Gloucestershire and another 10,000 by Hampshire. Other commodities known to have been procured were bacon, beans, cheese, flour, biscuits, galantine, wine, syrups and other consumables, almost all of which must have been for consumption by the crews, passengers and horses during the voyage to the Holy Land.

Logistics Ashore

It is often said that medieval armies 'lived off the land' and this may indeed have been possible for small armies in western Europe, with its abundance of agriculture, numerous farm animals, extensive grass-lands, and many rivers and streams. However, the same was much less practicable in the Holy Land and, although it may have been feasible on some occasions, the possibility that thousands of men could fan out each evening to find food, water and firewood for themselves, and fodder and water for their horses failed in practice. Naturally, there would have been some foraging and individual soldiers would have purloined any chickens or sheep, fruit or vegetables that they came across during the course of a march, as soldiers have always done, and some of these might also have been found in the immediate vicinity of a new campsite. Both men and horses would undoubtedly also have taken every opportunity to drink from any stream or river they encountered.

However, the leading elements on the march and the first into a new campsite would have quickly exhausted what little was available, leaving nothing at all for those further back down the column. Saladin regularly implemented a 'scorched earth' policy, demolishing buildings, carrying away foodstuffs and poisoning wells to prevent them from being used by either humans or animals. Of more immediate concern to the Crusaders was that Saracen horsemen were always hovering around the edges of their army, waiting to pounce on, and either kill or capture, any individual or group they could lay their hands on, which severely limited the opportunities for foraging. Crusader supply convoys were always a target, and getting the provisions from the supply bases to the troops was a constant problem, and always required a large escort.

Individual Consumption

Detailed records of the ration requirements of Crusader soldiers on campaign are non-existent, and Ambroise makes little mention of food, except when there were problems. Thus, just before the Battle of Arsuf in September 1191 he tells how 'there was a great throng on account of the horses who had died of their wounds; for the people were so eager to purchase the horse-flesh that they even had recourse to blows', while during the attempt to reach Jerusalem in December of that year, he refers to the storms which 'spoiled all the biscuits and bacon'. Extrapolating from accounts of peasant life in Europe, it seems reasonable to assume that the average Crusader's diet probably consisted of hard, dry biscuit, a soup of beans and a little salted pork or bacon, occasionally supplemented by fresh fruit, vegetables and horsemeat.

The nobility and knights would have moved their supplies by pack animals or carts, but the great mass of foot soldiers normally carried ten days' rations. On the occasion of the second march towards Jerusalem, however, 'the crowd of the lower class of people were so eager to proceed to Jerusalem that, made active by hope, they took the provision baggage on their shoulders, asserting that they were fully able to carry a month's supply.'

Food was eaten from wooden or clay bowls or plates, using a knife and spoon, or more probably in the case of the soldiers, their fingers. The commonest drinking vessels were wooden, pottery or leather mugs, and, possibly, animal horns. But, whatever implements they used, each man would have had to carry his own.

The fact that the men were required to carry ten days' supplies suggests that there was a recognised daily food allowance, but the only known record of a daily ration for the period is that for twelfth-century Venetian galley slaves. In Table II this is compared with three other

Table II: Comparison of Campaign Rations

Unit Year	Galley Slave ca.1200	Union Army 1862	British Army 1815	British Army 1914
Bread or biscuit	25 oz	16 oz	24 oz	16 oz
Cheese	1.4 oz	—	—	3 oz
Salted meat	2 oz	12 oz	16 oz	16 oz
Bacon	—	—	—	4 oz
Vegetables	3.5 oz	4 oz	32 oz	8 oz
Jam	—	—	—	4 oz
Sugar/Tea/ Coffee/Salt	—	4 oz	—	4 oz
TOTAL	2 lb	2.3 lb	4.5 lb	3.5 lb

The table shows the daily combat ration figures for twelfth-century galley slaves, the Union Army in the American Civil War, and the British Army in 1815 and 1914. The only one seriously out of line with the others is the British Army 1815 ration, which was due to a particularly lavish allowance of potatoes.

known figures of a later age, but before modern technology had introduced frozen and dehydrated rations.

We are not concerned here with the details of the Crusaders' diet but rather with the overall ration requirement. On the assumption that a Crusader soldier could not be given less than a galley slave, it would seem reasonable that the daily food requirement across the army as a whole was about 2 lb per man per day.

A further constant requirement for a medieval army was fuel, which was essential if food and water were to be heated and, albeit of lesser importance, to provide warmth during the worst of winter. Some use may have been made of animal dung, but the main requirement would have been for firewood, and there are several references in the Saracen texts to Crusaders collecting this. The only figure that can be found to give some guidance on quantities is that in nineteenth-century British India, a sepoy on campaign was entitled to two *seer* of firewood per day, which at the official conversion rate was 4.2 lb. It seems not unreasonable to set a figure of 1 lb per man per day for a medieval army.

This means that, using the ten days' requirement, the average foot soldier would have normally carried a ration load of 30 lb, which would have reduced by 3 lb per day until he was able to restock. Bearing in mind the rest of his load, including helmet, short sword, hauberk, some form of shield, eating utensils and a few spare clothes, this is a feasible amount. When the men volunteered to carry one month's provisions for the final march to Jerusalem, however, this would have amounted to 90 lb (i.e. 3 lb per day for thirty days) and despite their enthusiasm and religious fervour, this would have been at the very limit of the capabilities of most and beyond those of the weaker ones.

Water

Water was as essential to the Crusaders as to any other human being, both for drinking and for cooking, since the standard method of cooking their limited meat and vegetables was boiling to produce either a thin soup or a stew, or in combination with flour, to make biscuits. Modern armies take water supply very seriously and it has been proven time and again that lack of the required amount of water causes a rapid decline in an individual's ability to make decisions and to perform tasks efficiently. Thus, the current US Army planning figure is that for maximum efficiency when performing hard work in the sun at 43° C a person requires 4.2 gallons of water per day. Medieval soldiers would have had no scientific basis for calculating water requirements and were almost certainly used to considerably less than modern soldiers; nevertheless, they were aware that it was a basic requirement and the fact that Saladin's men had poisoned the wells around Jerusalem was a major factor in calling off the second advance to Jerusalem.

The water ration for a galley slave was 4 pints per day. It seems reasonable, therefore, to assume that a land-based soldier undergoing the hardships of marching, carrying a heavy load and fighting, all while wearing highly unsuitable clothing and in the heat of the Holy Land, would have required at the very least the same. Furthermore, although there is no evidence one way or the other on the subject, it seems unlikely that medieval soldiers would have had an equivalent of the modern individual water-bottle and it is more probable that water would have been carried in animal skins by porters or in barrels on horse-drawn carts.

Horses

Feeding and watering the horses was a major preoccupation for any army up to the early twentieth century, and for the Crusaders gathering fodder was fraught with danger. A typical report recorded:

> ... on the sixth day after the feast of All Saints (7 November 1192), the esquires and men-at-arms went out to get fodder for their horses and beasts of burden. The Templars were guarding the esquires whilst they dispersed to find fresh herbage, a duty which sometimes cost them dear if they acted without much caution.

Medieval knights may have been uneducated and unsophisticated by today's standards, but they were driven by much the same imperatives. Thus, horses were absolutely vital for war, both for fighting and for general transportation and load carrying, while at all other times they were an essential symbol of social status. Horses would put up with great hardships, but if they were to function correctly it was essential that they should be looked after, which included, above all, being properly fed and watered.

The Crusaders had four types of horse, at the highest level being the *destrier,* a well-bred, highly-trained and very expensive stallion, affordable only to the nobility and the wealthiest knights. The heaviest horses of their time, their strength was needed to carry the knight and his armour, while their mass increased the shock effect of the knight and his spear when they impacted on an enemy either in combat or in a tournament. Modern descendants, such as the Belgian and the English Shire horses, weigh between 1,800 and 2,400 lb.

Next came the *courser,* a strong, steady, long-winded cavalry horse, which was neither as refined, nor as heavy as a destrier, but was much more widely available and affordable for the majority of knights. Their nearest modern equivalent is the heavy dragoon horse of the nineteenth century, which had a weight of about 1,300–1,500 lb. Some coursers were specifically bred for speed, in order to carry messengers either between royal courts or between elements of an army in the field. The third type was the *palfrey*, a short-legged, long-bodied horse, weighing about 1,000 lb, which gave a much more comfortable ride, but was certainly not fast; this was used for normal riding and travelling. Finally, came the *rouncey*, a general-purpose animal used for riding by the knight's servants or as a pack animal.

The planning figures for the consumption by horses on medieval campaigns cannot be discovered, but some more recent examples are given in Table III.

It seems a reasonable assumption that at the time of the Third Crusade an *average* horse would have been a little smaller than today's equivalents and that the daily ration requirements would have been

Table III: Examples of Daily Rations for Horses

Source	Work Level	Daily Ration
Peninsular War (1808–14)[1]	—	20–26 lb
France 1815[2]	Heavy[4]	25 lb
	Light[5]	20 lb
US National Research Council[3]	Intense	24–36 lb
	Moderate	21–30 lb
	Light	18–24 lb

1 Laid down in Wellington's General Orders.

2 Laid down in Peace Treaty, 1815.

3 Contemporary figures for a mature 1,200 lb horse.

4 Officers' saddle horses, cavalry horses, and artillery horses drawing guns.

5 All other horses, except that on a march exceeding four days all horses received the 'heavy ration'.

correspondingly less. Thus, for the purposes of this book, a planning figure for the daily ration requirement of solids for the average horse is taken to be 15 lb per day when idle and 20 lb per day when active.

Every knight would have aimed to have an absolute minimum of three horses: a destrier for combat, a courser or palfrey for routine riding and a rouncey for use as a pack animal. Wealthier knights had more and it is clear that Richard had a large stock of horses; for example, on one occasion he offered to give a live horse to any knight who would donate his dead one to the starving foot soldiers. There were also pack-horses and mules – 'beasts of burthen' – in the supply train. Losses in horses were considerable, both in combat and from hunger, thirst and illness, and sometimes knights were reduced to riding donkeys or even to walking. The only sources of replacements were remounts from abroad, capture from the Saracens, or in a few cases, purchase from owners who had decided to return home. It seems reasonable to assume that, at any one time, there was an average across the army as a whole, including the 'beasts of burthen', of three horses per knight.

At Sea

Sea voyages were hazardous undertakings for both humans and horses in medieval times, and conditions for the horses were doubtless much harsher than they would be today. One of the greatest problems was that the horses were usually accommodated in the hold and in medieval ships the hatches were normally battened down in anything except the mildest weather, which restricted ventilation. Thus, deaths due to asphyxiation were added to those due to sickness, disease and general debilitation. However, even in those unsophisticated times, the practical requirement was that the ship's master had to deliver a reasonable number of live horses at the destination, so the customary method of payment was a fixed sum for every horse embarked, plus a further fixed sum for every live horse delivered.

There is a lack of contemporary information concerning a horse's requirements at sea, but two examples have been found regarding shipboard rations for cavalry units sailing to South Africa 1899–1903. In the first, a cavalryman recommends an average of 15–18 lb per horse per day, while in the second, a professional veterinarian recommends the somewhat higher figure of 19–27 lb. It appears reasonable to assume that the veterinarian would have been more generous than the pragmatic cavalryman, so it is suggested that a reasonable average for Crusader times would be 15 lb per horse per day, which agrees with the figure derived for land-based horses when undertaking light work.

Water

The second major consumable for horses, whether on land or at sea, was water and most modern authorities agree on a daily figure of 1 gallon per 100 lb of body weight. For an average 1,200 lb horse this results in a requirement of some 12 gallons of water per day, which increases in high ambient temperatures or at a time of great activity and decreases when a horse is idle or relatively inactive. Making allowances for medieval horses being smaller and less well looked after, a figure of 5 gallons per day seems reasonable.

Assessing the Numbers

To summarise, the suggested *daily* planning figures are:

> **Men**: Food/fuel – 3 lb and water – 4 pints per man.
> **Horses**: Fodder/forage – 15 lb and water – 5 gallons per horse.

Having established the figures for consumption, it is now necessary to consider the actual numbers involved, although there are no surviving accounting documents such as muster rolls, quittance rolls (records of individual payments), or masters' logs for the ships (which would give the number, if not the names, of passengers). Thus, in order to assess the scale of logistical support required by Richard's army it is necessary to estimate the numbers involved.

Medieval writers do give figures, but there can be little doubt that in the case of the larger numbers they were simply very wild guesses. During the march from Acre to Jaffa in August–September 1191, for example, Ambroise says that the Christian army 'did not exceed 100,000', while at Arsuf he records that 'an innumerable host of Turks, reckoned at 300,000, covered the face of the whole land'. This figure of 300,000 appears several times elsewhere, for example for the number of Crusader dead at Acre, and it seems safe to conclude that it simply means 'a very large number'. Similarly, Ambroise records that once the Battle of Arsuf had started, 'there appeared a large body of the Turks, ten thousand strong, coming down on us at full charge'. Nobody on the receiving end of a cavalry charge could possibly make an accurate count and in this case the writer clearly means 'a large number'.

The difficulties associated with assessing the numbers in a crowd is by no means unknown today. It is relatively easy to estimate the size of a crowd in a sports stadium, since the number of tickets sold can be counted, but for a crowd on the streets or in an open space it is quite a different matter. In 2001, for example, one particular demonstration in London was described by the march organisers as over 50,000 strong, but as well under 30,000 by the police, while at a separate occasion during Queen Elizabeth II's Jubilee celebrations on 2 June 2002, the crowd on the Mall was said to be one million strong which, at the very best, can be no more than an educated guess.

However, there are reports in the Third Crusade of some smaller numbers that might be more meaningful. For example, when discussing a possible attack on Egypt, Richard offered to pay the French for 700 knights and 2,000 of their followers, and there seems little doubt that his accountants would have ensured that the right numbers were selected and paid for. Similarly, when the remaining French left Richard's army at Easter 1192 Ambroise states that there were '700 knights, proven men of valour' which, again, seems a believable figure, and is also consistent with Richard's earlier offer. It is suggested, therefore, that numbers below 1,000 may be cautiously accepted, but above that they should be regarded with a suspicion which increases in direct proportion to the number given.

A further difficulty is that where actual numbers are mentioned, it is clear that, with only the rarest exceptions, the only people who were of any importance to contemporary chroniclers were the knights. All except the very poorest knights, however, would have had an esquire, a groom and at least one servant, while the better off would have had considerably more. In addition, there were men-at-arms, sappers, artillerymen (for ballistae, etc.), bowmen, bowyers, fletchers, pack-horse and cart drivers, blacksmiths, sutlers, priests and laundrywomen, while numbers of pilgrims are also known to have accompanied the army in the hope of reaching Jerusalem. It is considered that a reasonable proportion, taken across the army as a whole, would be nine 'others' to every one knight.

Composition of the Crusader Army

The army of the Third Crusade was made up of five major and many minor contingents, the two largest being those supplied by King Richard of England and King Philip of France. The third element was the force of Outremer, i.e. the descendants of Christians who had settled in the

Holy Land after the First and Second Crusades, most of whom had been expelled from their homes by Saladin's army following the Battle of Hattin. This included men from the Kingdom of Jerusalem, the County of Tripoli and the Principality of Antioch. The other two major elements were the two great military orders, the Hospitallers and the Templars, both of which had suffered grievous losses at the Battle of Hattin, but had since received reinforcements from their members in Europe. That they had significant numbers is clear from the fact that they took it in turns to provide the van and rearguards on all marches. Also, in addition to the mounted knights, their numbers included sergeants, turcopoles and mercenaries.

There were also a significant number of smaller contingents, Ambroise remarking that 'all the nations of Europe were represented'. Among those known to have been present were a combined Danish/ Norwegian contingent, a Hungarian contingent, and two Italian contingents, one from Genoa and the other from Pisa. Some of the survivors of Barbarossa's ill-fated Holy Roman Empire expedition, possibly as many as a thousand, were at the siege of Acre, where they were initially led by Friedrich von Schwaben. When he died during the siege, Duke Leopold of Austria took command, but went home after being insulted by Richard. Presumably, most of his compatriots went with him, but a few appear to have remained and there was certainly a German knight named Henry at Richard's side when he entered Jaffa on 5 August 1192. Finally, there were numbers of mercenaries from both Europe and the Middle East, two groups mentioned in the various chronicles being bedouin and miners from Aleppo.

The fleet which brought Richard's army to the Holy Land consisted of about 200 ships with an average capacity of eighty passengers; thus, the English contingent could not have numbered more than 16,000 and was probably somewhat less. There would have been some losses in the siege of

Acre, while Richard undoubtedly left some men to garrison Cyprus and others to garrison Acre. It would appear reasonable to estimate that the English contingent on the march to Jaffa was 9,000 of which 900 were cavalry. The French contingent was almost certainly slightly smaller than that of England; say, 7,000 of which 700 were cavalry.

There were, of course, losses. Men were killed or captured by the Saracens, and there were further deaths due to illness and exhaustion, while absence in Jaffa or Acre was also a problem of some significance. Saracen texts also make reference to desertions, but on what scale is not known. These were offset, albeit to an unknown extent, by the arrival of new Crusaders from Europe plus others who were rounded up in the various clear-outs of the 'idle ones' in the rear areas.

The Logistics of the March From Acre to Jaffa

It is now possible to take, as an example, the march from Acre to Jaffa, which has been described in detail in Chapter 5, but which is summarised in Table IV.

Assuming that the numbers involved were as shown in Table V and at daily consumption rates (food plus fuel) of 3 lb per man and 15 lb per horse, the requirement would have been $(20,000 \times 3) + (6,000 \times 15) = 150,000$ lb (67 tons) of solids per day. The total for the whole twenty days was, therefore, 1,340 tons. The men started with ten days' rations per man, which were almost exhausted when the ships made their first replenishment at Athlit on Day 8. Why a second replenishment should have been necessary two days later is not clear; it is possible that all the ships could not get ashore or that the unloading and distribution could not be completed in the first day. But, whatever the reason, the entire army should have been topped up to the ten-day figure by the time they left Caesarea on Day 11.

It is clear from contemporary accounts that the men were very short of food by about Day 18/19 and it is easy to see why. The Battle of Arsuf and the day of recovery which followed were presumably not in Richard's movement plan, as a result of which the ten days' rations were running out and the men were becoming very hungry, with their rations actually expiring as they reached Jaffa.

The water requirement was 4 pints per man and 5 gallons per horse, a total of 40,000 gallons (180 tons) per day. Thus, the total required for the whole march was 800,000 gallons (3,600 tons). Some of this would have come from local rivers and streams, but most would have had to be carried in the baggage train.

The figures for food and fuel have been expressed in terms of a particular quantity per man per day, which is the only way such planning can be conducted. However, while modern troops are given one pack containing the required rations for one day and overall quantities are thus easy to calculate, in medieval times matters would have been very much less precise and questions of what constituted a daily ration or a ten-day load are open to a wide variety of interpretations. Furthermore, medieval soldiers were considerably less disciplined and what could have sufficed one man for ten days might have lasted another for only six or seven days.

Conclusions

These calculations suggest, in the first instance, that a realistic figure for the strength of the army was in the region of 20,000 men and 6,000 horses. This is very considerably less than all contemporary and many modern estimates and it is acknowledged that it involves some sweeping generalisations and major assumptions. Nevertheless, it is suggested that these are still very large figures and if all these were to be concentrated into a marching column, as they were on the march from Acre to Jaffa,

Table IV: The Crusader March Acre–Jaffa

Date	Day	Event	Overnight	Miles Marched	Rations Carried	Other Events
Tuesday 20 August	-2	Orders for the move to Jaffa issued	Acre	—	—	
Thursday 22 August	1	March: Acre–River Belus	South bank of River Belus	2	10	Crossed river
Friday 23 August	2	March: River Belus–campsite	Campsite	2	9	Richard forces some elements of army out of Acre
Saturday 24 August	3	Rest	Campsite	0	8	
Sunday 25 August	4	March to Caiaphas	Caiaphas	11	7	
Monday 26 August	5	Rest	Caiaphas	0	6	Shed much baggage
Tuesday 27 August	6	March: Caiaphas–Athlit	Athlit	12	5	i. Route lies around Carmel peninsula ii. Midday halt at Capernaum
Wednesday 28 August	7	Rest	Athlit	0	4	Richard goes on ahead to Merla
Thursday 29 August	8	Rest/replenish	Athlit	0	3	Replenished from sea
Friday 30 August	9	March: Athlit–Merla	Merla	13	5	
Saturday 31 August	10	March: Merla–Caesarea[1]	Caesarea	3	4	Resupply from sea. Fleet brings reinforcements
Sunday 1 September	11	March: Caesarea–Dead River.	Dead River	3	10	i. Much fighting ii Camped on south bank of river
Monday 2 September	12	Rest	Dead River	0	9	
Tuesday 3 September	13	March: Dead River–Salt River	Salt River	7	8	Forced to move to inland road

Date	Day	Event	Overnight	Miles Marched	Rations Carried	Other Events
Wednesday 4 September	14	Rest	Salt River	0	7	
Thursday 5 September	15	Main body marches Salt River– River Rochetaillie	River Rochetaillie	10	6	i. Richard meets Saphadin for truce discussions ii. Through Forest of Arsuf
Friday 6 September	16	Rest	River Rochetaillie	0	5	
Saturday 7 September	17	March: River Rochetaillie–Arsuf	Arsuf	6	4	Major battle
Sunday 8 September	18	Recovery after battle	Arsuf	0	3	
Monday 9 September	19	March: Arsuf–River al-Awjah	River al-Awjah	6	2	
Tuesday 10 September	20	March: River al-Awjah–Jaffa	Jaffa	5	1	
TOTAL	20			80		

1 From here on, at least some elements of the fleet kept pace with the army.

Table V: Richard's Army: Acre–Jaffa
(estimates)

Army	Cavalry	Foot	TOTAL	Horses
English	900	8,100	9,000	2,700
French	700	6,300	7,000	2,100
Military Knights	200	1,800	2,000	600
Outremer	100	900	1,000	300
Others	100	900	1,000	300
TOTAL	2,000	18,000	20,000	6,000

for example, they would take a very long time to pass a given point. Similarly, when they occupied a campsite, they must have taken up a very considerable area. In either case, they would have appeared to an observer to constitute a massive force.

Having accepted the figures for the men and horses, and again making some major assumptions, the calculations show that Richard's army would have consumed some 67 tons of solids every day, and 1,340 tons over the twenty-day march. It should be noted that this is a figure for consumption and simply means that this amount had to come from somewhere. However, the close proximity of the Saracens throughout the march and their attacks on anyone who became separated from the main body, restricted the prospects for foraging almost to zero, although the rivers and streams would have provided at least some of the water requirements. Nevertheless, the figure is large and only a reasonably sophisticated and effective logistical plan, coupled with disciplined implementation, could have enabled such a large body to move with comparatively small problems from Acre to Jaffa.

Once again, it is clear that Richard learned from Vegetius, who said that:

> Famine makes greater havoc in an army than the enemy, and is more terrible than the sword. Time and opportunity may help to retrieve other misfortunes, but where forage and provisions have not been carefully provided, the evil is without remedy.

CHAPTER 13

Richard I as a Military Commander

Richard I was commander of the English army and fleet throughout the Third Crusade, from leaving England in 1190 until his departure from the Holy Land in October 1192. In addition, he was the joint commander with King Philip Augustus of France of the Crusader army, from June 1191 until the latter's departure on 31 July 1191. Thereafter, Richard was the undisputed commander-in-chief until his own departure in October 1192. During that period he conquered Cyprus in an independent campaign, was the joint victor at the siege of Acre and then conducted a series of mobile operations, which included one short, sharp siege, two pitched battles, a succession of long marches, numerous skirmishes and an almost endless series of personal combats. As a general he was never defeated in the field, and as a warrior he suffered only a few, relatively minor wounds.

At the time of Richard's arrival in 1191, Saladin controlled the entire territory of the Kingdom of Jerusalem, including, most importantly (from the Crusaders' point of view), the Holy City itself. He also held all the coastline, with the exception of a few scattered outposts and a small stretch of land containing the Crusader army besieging Acre. By 1190, Saladin's army had become accustomed to success and it seemed that it would not be long before the last few Crusader outposts in Outremer, including Tyre, would be rolled-up. Following this, the only two other remaining Western territories – the Principality of Antioch and the County of Tripoli – would be finished off, thus bringing the entire Crusader enterprise to an inglorious end. To add to the Crusaders' woes, the question of the kingship of Jerusalem was a matter of bitter and seemingly endless dispute. By the time of Richard's departure, however, a three-year truce was in place, the Crusaders controlled the entire coastline as far south as Darum, except for Ascalon which had been demilitarised, and there was an undisputed King of Jerusalem, although the Holy City itself remained tantalisingly just out of reach. But the Third Crusade's primary mission had always been crystal clear – it was to regain the Holy City of Jerusalem – and this was never achieved.

Richard as a Strategist

The single aim of the vast majority of the Crusaders – indeed, the only reason they had volunteered for such great hardship – was to reach the Holy City. It is difficult in modern times to appreciate just how important and inspiring this was to medieval men and women. Even most of those who had settled in the Holy Land and then lost their land to Saladin seemed to agree that this was a greater priority than regaining their own homes.

The distance from Jaffa to Jerusalem is not great and on each of their two attempts to reach it the Crusaders got within a close distance of their goal, but turned back both times. Richard, as commander-in-chief, must shoulder a large part of the responsibility, and it was known throughout the Crusader army that Richard was very averse to going the last few miles to take Jerusalem. However, it may not have been evident to them that his reasons were not idly given, but were the result of deep, rational consideration and a very careful and objective assessment of the risks involved. It is also the case that on both occasions the matter was thoroughly discussed by an advisory council and that each time these councils recommended a withdrawal.

In planning those final drives, Richard foresaw a number of major problems. He had to plan for the possibility that the siege of Jerusalem would be long and drawn out. Subsequent reports from the Saracen side make it clear that there was panic in the city at the news of the Crusaders' approach, but there is no reason to suppose that, in the final analysis, Saladin would not have tried to hold. Therefore, as Richard pointed out, the Crusader army would have to surround the city, fight off any Saracen army coming to the aid of its comrades, and keep open a line of communication some 80 miles long, none of which would be an easy task. Furthermore, unlike the siege at Acre, the Crusaders would not have a reasonably secure seaborne line of communication with the outside world.

If they were to succeed in taking the city, a great but unpredictable number of the Crusaders would consider that they had achieved their aim and fulfilled their vows, and would then be only too eager to go home again. This would leave only a small garrison to protect their gains from the Saracens. Taking the city would mean that although they had defeated the enemy garrison, they would not have defeated the main Saracen army. That army, probably still led by Saladin, would continue to dominate the countryside in a way which the Crusaders, with their very limited manpower, never could. This would inevitably leave the city as a Crusader outpost and all Saladin would have to do would be to close the route to the coast and wait for the city to fall, like a ripe plum, into his hands. Richard recognised that he did not have an army that was sufficiently strong to undertake the task, even when it was acting together, and it is difficult to avoid the conclusion that he was right.

Battles

Richard never once sought a set-piece battle with Saladin, and the greatest confrontation between the two leaders was at Arsuf, which was fought on ground and at a time entirely of the Saracen commander's own choosing. Furthermore, Richard only undertook sieges of his own volition when he was confident of a quick resolution, as at Darum. Without a doubt, Richard's greatest military skills were in mobile warfare, and in very rapid reactions to a sudden threat, as in the attack on the caravan near La Galatie and the retaking of Jaffa.

Military Problems

One of Richard's most fundamental considerations was that he commanded the only existing operational Crusader field army. Thus, if it was defeated, not only would the western Christians have to raise yet another completely new army (if indeed they were willing to do so) but that army would have to start the conquest of the Holy Land from scratch. Thus, at the very least, Richard had to maintain that army in existence. The army that he did have was made up of a number of disparate elements and his control over them was by no means absolute, except in the case of the contingents from his own country, and those who were prepared to swear allegiance to him – usually in exchange for money.

Medieval armies were almost always ill-disciplined, but despite the large numbers of different nationalities, Richard seems to have been able to impose his will during the marches and battles. In particular, during the march from Acre to Jaffa and the Battle of Arsuf, he succeeded in forcing the men to behave in a very disciplined manner. His particular problem was with the knights, whose sole desire was always to charge straight for the enemy and to engage them in close-quarter combat, regardless of the risks. Unfortunately, this made them easy victims for the Saracens, who repeatedly tempted small parties of such knights to fall into ambushes and exacted a small if steady toll of men killed, wounded, or taken away as slaves.

One way Richard imposed tactical discipline was to separate his army into divisions and squadrons, with clearly designated commanders, so that the chain-of-command and responsibilities were clearly understood. Unlike many contemporary commanders who put their entire force into battle simultaneously, Richard also maintained a reserve, which could be used either to reinforce a threatened portion of the line in order to prevent an enemy breakthrough, or to take advantage of an enemy weakness.

The Crusader army had as effective a communications system as was possible in the circumstances. The main rallying point was always indicated by the huge mobile tower carrying the king's banner, its height guaranteeing that it would be seen from any point on the battlefield. Communications between commanders were by couriers and instructions to the army as a whole were given by trumpeters.

Although he never spelt it out, Richard's actions demonstrate some reluctance to get too far from the sea. Firstly, his ships always provided him with a guaranteed supply line, whether from Tyre, Acre, Cyprus or western Europe. Secondly, however, it may also have been in his mind that the sea gave him an escape route to extract his English army, should that ever become necessary, a factor which has weighed heavily with English com- . manders engaged in overseas operations down the succeeding centuries.

As discussed in Chapter 12, it is difficult to establish the actual strength of the Crusader army with any degree of confidence. One thing that is certain, however, is that the number of effectives available to Richard in the field was always very considerably less than the number of Crusaders actually in the Holy Land. This was due, in part, to the departures, from time to time, of the French contingent, but was also a result of the need to leave garrisons in castles and towns, and to provide large escorts for convoys. There was also a large amount of sickness, which could be expected in any medieval campaign. In addition to these, Richard was plagued by the problem of 'internal desertion'; i.e. men who did not (or were unable to) leave the country, but who chose to stay in the fleshpots on the coast rather than go on campaign with the field army. Therefore, many men remained in Acre during the time when their comrades were flogging their way along the coast to Jaffa, and more remained in both Acre and Jaffa during the attempts to reach Jerusalem. The chroniclers do not give either their nationality or numbers, but that they represented a significant loss is borne out by the amount of times Richard sent various high-ranking emissaries to those towns to persuade them to report back for duty; indeed, on at least one occasion he had to go himself.

The maps of the era were rudimentary in the extreme, but some did exist, and Richard was certainly given one depicting the layout of the city of Jerusalem. To what extent he had any knowledge of the topography of the rest of the country is not clear, although it is known that he relied heavily on the military knights and local residents. Certainly, he conquered Cyprus, whose topography was almost totally unknown to him and other members of his English army, and the route and the halts on the march from Acre to Jaffa were well-planned, suggesting that such oral sources were reasonably accurate. In June 1192, Richard and his men made their spectacular ride through the night, first to a rendezvous with their supplies and then on to find and attack a Saracen caravan near La Galatie, which was almost certainly done with the aid of bedouin guides.

One aspect of Richard's military character which needs to be touched upon is the frequent reports of the king issuing bloodcurdling threats to the effect that he would behead or torture his men if they failed in their duty. Two specific examples were during the sea battle against the Saracen dromon and at the Battle of Jaffa. These are, indeed, some commanders who find it necessary to issue such threats due to their own inadequacies, but Richard was not one of them. These threats were always followed by renewed efforts by his men, but it is doubtful that the threats were anything other than rhetorical and immediately recognised as such by his troops, who, in all probability, greeted them with a wry smile. There is certainly not a single reported instance of him having carried out any – nor, indeed, of needing to.

Political Problems

In addition to their military challenges, all commanders-in-chief must expect to face some political problems, but Richard certainly had more than his fair share, of which the most consistently troublesome was his relationship with the French. This was due, in part, to historical reasons, since Richard was duke of both Normandy and Aquitaine, as well as Count of Anjou, and thus ruled over a large part of what many other Frenchmen considered to be their national territory. Richard had sworn fealty to Philip, but this did not mean a great deal, and both Richard and his father had fought several campaigns against the French king. A second reason was that Richard was far wealthier than Philip, which meant that the French king and later the Duke of Burgundy, repeatedly had to go to the English king to ask for either financial aid, the provision of military equipment or a share in the spoils, major humiliations for such proud men.

There is no doubt that a large proportion of the French in the Holy

Land were very shaken by the sudden departure of their king in July 1191; he had been ill, but so had almost everyone else, including Richard, and it appeared to them as if their king had abandoned them, leaving the King of England in indisputable command. During their time together in Sicily and at the siege of Acre, the English king had consistently outshone his French counterpart, and Richard was clearly a warrior enjoying, indeed revelling in, campaigning, none of which applied to Philip. In addition, Richard had a charismatic personality and could inspire his troops both by his words and by his deeds, whether as a general who clearly cared for his men, as a warrior who would take on any opponent in single combat, or as a man who would join them in carrying rocks or baulks of timber. Philip's motives for his departure were probably a mixture of a wish to escape daily contact with Richard and a desire to get home in order to pursue his territorial ambitions in western Europe while Richard was detained in the Holy Land. Whatever they were, the act left a bad taste in the mouths of his compatriots who he left behind.

Where the kingship of Jerusalem was concerned, it was, perhaps, more an accident of history and family relationships rather than by design that the French seemed fated to take the opposite view to Richard on the question of the succession. In particular, their support for the arrogant and erratic Conrad of Montferrat was always a problem for Richard.

The French also mistrusted Richard because of his repeated negotiations with the Saracens, which started almost as soon as he landed at Acre. The French saw this as inevitably compromising the aim of the Crusade, whereas Richard, a much more pragmatic man, saw diplomacy as a second element in his campaign. Nevertheless, this French mistrust of Richard's negotiations did not prevent them from encouraging Conrad from doing so, as well.

Finally, and most fundamentally, the French consistently disagreed with Richard over the strategic direction of the campaign. They were always pushing him to march to the Holy City and lay siege to it, and seemed either unable or unwilling to consider his carefully thought-out reasons for not doing so. The Duke of Burgundy took this to the point where he twice agreed to the formation of a council to consider the issue and then, when the council recommended abandoning the march on Jerusalem, refused to accept its verdict.

There can be no doubt that Richard was often a difficult man to get on with, and the charges that he was arrogant and sometimes inconsiderate to his allies obviously had some justification. However, the problem was that he and the French were bound together: the French needed him for his money and generalship, while he needed them for their numbers and their military qualities.

Conrad of Montferrat was another constant irritant. He had arrived at Tyre at a critical point during its siege by Saladin and had so inspired the defence that the citizens chose him as their leader, and Saladin decided to seek easier conquests elsewhere. Once he possessed this secure base, Conrad's ambitions and arrogance knew few bounds. He refused to allow King Guy to enter Tyre and use it as his royal capital, and caused incessant difficulties for Richard, particularly by encouraging the rift between the French contingent and the English king. He even conducted quite separate negotiations with Saladin, in which Conrad's sole desire was to ensure his own position, rather than to promote the well-being of the Crusader army.

Last, but by no means the least, of Richard's political problems was the situation in his own kingdom. He received several reports telling him that, despite all the promises made prior to his brother's departure, Prince John was assuming ever greater powers, and that corruption was rife. Further, Richard was told that King Philip was ignoring the treaty he had signed immediately prior to his departure and was posing an increasingly dangerous threat to Richard's domains. Every one of these letters begged Richard to return home as soon as possible, and this pressure had an undoubted impact on him and his ability to concentrate on affairs in the Holy Land.

Finale

When Richard sailed away in October 1192 he left behind him a three-year truce which had, in effect, ratified the reduction of the Kingdom of Jerusalem to a colony and confirmed Saladin's suzerainty over the entire area. In the north, the Principality of Antioch and County of Tripoli, which had successfully stood apart from the main activities of the Third Crusade, nevertheless lacked depth and were in essence coastal strips hemmed in by potentially hostile states. The kingdom itself was also a coastal strip – barely 10 miles wide in places, but stretching inland as far as Lydda and Ramla in others – and consisted mainly of the fortified strongholds at Tyre, Acre, Caiaphas and Jaffa. There was at last a king of Jerusalem to be sure, but his kingdom was in most respects a fiction and Henry only lived for another three years before being killed in an accident when he fell out of a high window onto a courtyard,[15] leaving Queen Isabella yet again in need of someone with whom to share the throne.[16]

Where Richard's constant involvement in personal combat is concerned it is difficult to argue with Saladin's view that Richard was 'imprudent, not to say foolishly so, in thrusting himself so frequently into great danger, and shows too great recklessness of his own life.' Indeed, such was the frequency of his personal adventures that it is difficult to see how he got away as lightly as he did, with just a few cuts and bruises, although all observers on both sides agree that he was a quite exceptional fighting man. Perhaps his finest moment as a tactician was in the defence of Jaffa against Saladin's final attack, when he formed a 'thin red line' of infantry and somehow managed to be everywhere at once, until the Saracen defeat was assured.

In very marked contrast to his performance as a fighter, however, Richard was an extremely prudent and careful commander. He regularly carried out what would today be termed 'risk assessments' and carefully identified and then weighed up all the factors before reaching a decision. He moved his army from England and western France to the Holy Land and maintained it there for just under two years, the furthest 'overseas deployment' ever undertaken by an English king up to that time.

Unlike many commanders, he paid scrupulous attention to logistics, and while his men and horses were sometimes on short commons, they never actually starved. He was particularly reluctant to attempt the siege of Jerusalem because he foresaw, almost certainly correctly, that his lines of communication to the coast, upon which his army was entirely dependant, would either be cut, or he would have to devote so many troops to keeping them open that he would not be able to besiege and take Jerusalem. Indeed, this could have led to a major military disaster. He also paid considerable attention – within the limitations of contemporary knowledge – to the well-being, morale and medical treatment of his troops.

The march from Acre to Jaffa, the Battle of Arsuf, the attack on the convoy and the Battle of Jaffa were all tactical masterpieces and fully merit Richard's inclusion in the gallery of great commanders. That Richard did not achieve his strategic aim of taking Jerusalem is no less a measure of his greatness and sophistication, since generals also require the moral courage to avoid placing inadequate forces in jeopardy from which there will be no escape.

Vegetius's *De Re Militari*

Like his father, Henry II, Richard I was an avid disciple of the work *De Re Militari*, and is reputed to have carried a copy with him on all his campaigns. This book, written by Flavius Vegetius Renatus for the Emperor Valentinian II in about 390 AD, was a compilation of the military wisdom and customs of the Romans and remained the single most influential military work in the western world for well over one and a half millennia. For the first thousand years or so it circulated in manuscript form, first in Latin, but later also translated into English and French, and at least 150 of these copies remain in various libraries and archives. Then, albeit well after the time of Richard I, the invention of printing in the late fifteenth century encouraged translations into other languages as well, including Dutch, German and Italian, with Caxton's first English edition appearing in 1489.

Over this period *De Re Militari* was the only available dissertation on the art of war and served as a combination of strategic primer and field service pocket book. Little is known about Vegetius himself, except that it appears that he was not a soldier – what he sought to do was draw on and

distil ancient manuscripts and regulations in order to describe the operations and structure of the army that had made Rome such a great
power.

Vegetius's book is divided into four sections, which deal in some
detail with various aspects of war, and some of his teachings are as true
today as when he wrote them. For example, 'he who aspires to peace
should prepare for war'; 'discipline is more important than numbers';
and 'few men are born brave, but many become so through training and
discipline'.

At the end of Book III he summarises his work in a number of
'maxims' which give the general flavour of his teachings:[17]

It is the nature of war that what is beneficial to you is detrimental to the
enemy and what is of service to him always hurts you. It is therefore a
maxim never to do, or to omit doing, anything as a consequence of his
actions, but to consult invariably your own interest only. And you depart
from this interest whenever you imitate such measures as he pursues for his
benefit. For the same reason it would be wrong for him to follow such steps
as you take for your advantage.

The more your troops have been accustomed to camp duties on frontier
stations and the more carefully they have been disciplined, the less danger
they will be exposed to in the field.

Men must be sufficiently tried before they are led against the enemy.

It is much better to overcome the enemy by famine, surprise or terror than
by general actions (i.e. battles), for in the latter instance fortune has often a
greater share than valour. Those designs are best which the enemy are
entirely ignorant of till the moment of execution. Opportunity in war is
often more to be depended on than courage.

To encourage the enemy's soldiers to desert is of especial service, for an adversary is more hurt by desertion than by slaughter.

It is better to have several bodies of reserves than to extend your front too much.

A general is not easily overcome who can form a true judgement of his own and the enemy's forces.

Valour is superior to numbers.

The nature of the ground is often of more consequence than courage.

Few men are born brave; many become so through care and force of discipline.

An army is strengthened by labour and enervated by idleness.

Troops are not to be led to battle unless confident of success.

Novelty and surprise throw an enemy into consternation; but common incidents have no effect.

He who rashly pursues a flying enemy with his own troops in disorder, seems inclined to resign that victory which he had before obtained.

An army unsupplied with grain and other necessary provisions will be vanquished without striking a blow.

A general who trusts to his cavalry should choose the proper ground for them and employ them principally in the action.

He who depends on his infantry should choose a situation most proper for them and make most use of their service.

When an enemy's spy lurks in the camp, order all your soldiers in the day time to their tents, and he will instantly be apprehended.

On finding the enemy has notice of your designs, you must immediately alter your plan of operations.

Consult with many on proper measures to be taken, but communicate the plans you intend to put in execution to few, and those only of the most assured fidelity; or rather trust no one but yourself.

Punishment, and fear thereof, are necessary to keep soldiers in order in quarters; but in the field they are more influenced by hope and rewards.

Good generals never engage in battles unless induced by opportunity or obliged by necessity.

To distress the enemy more by famine than the sword is a mark of consummate skill.

Many instructions might be given with regard to the cavalry. But as this branch of the service has been brought to perfection since the ancient writers and considerable improvements have been made in their drills and manoeuvres, their arms, and the quality and management of their horses, nothing can be collected from their works. Our present mode of discipline is sufficient.

Dispositions for action must be carefully concealed from the enemy, lest they should counteract them and defeat your plans by proper expedients.

Richard I in His Own Words

I. The Disciplinary Code for Richard's fleet
Issued at Chinon in Anjou, June 1190.

Richard, by the grace of God king of England, duke of Normandy and Aquitaine, and Count of Anjou, to all his men who are about to journey to Jerusalem by sea – health.

Know that with the common counsel of approved men we have had the following regulations drawn up. Whoever on board ship shall slay another is himself to be cast into the sea lashed to the dead man; if he have slain him ashore he is to be buried in the same way. If anyone be proved by worthy witnesses to have drawn a knife for the purpose of striking another, or to have wounded another so as to draw blood, let him lose his fist; but if he strike another with his hand and draw no blood, let him be dipped three times in the sea. If anyone cast reproach or bad word against another, or invoke God's malison [a curse] on him, let him for every offence pay an ounce of silver. Let a convicted thief be shorn like a prize-fighter; after which let boiling pitch be poured on his head and a feather pillow be shaken over it so as to make him a laughing-stock. Then let him be put ashore at the first land where the ships touch.

Witness myself at Chinon.

II. A letter home, reporting on the march from Acre to Jaffa

A personal letter written at Jaffa on 1 October 1191.

Richard by the grace of God king of England, duke of Normandy and Aquitaine, and Count of Anjou, to N. his beloved and faithful [servant], sends his greeting.

Know that after the taking of Acre and the departure of the king of France, who there, against the will of God and to the eternal dishonour of his kingdom, so shamelessly failed in his vow, we set out for Joppa (Jaffa). And as we were nearing Arsuf Saladin came fiercely swooping down upon us. But, of God's mercy, we lost no man of importance that day, saving one only – James de Avesnes – a man right dearly beloved by the whole army; and rightly so too, for he had proved himself, by many years' service in the Christian host, to be vigorous, devout, and, as it were, a very column [of support] in holiness and sincerity of word. Thence by God's will we came to Joppa [Jaffa], which we have fortified with ditch and wall in our desire to do everything that can promote the Christian cause. On that day, to wit on the Vigil of the Nativity of the Blessed Mary, Saladin lost an infinite number of his greatest men; and being put to flight, in the absence of all help and counsel, he has laid waste the whole land of Syria. On the third day before Saladin's defeat we were ourselves wounded with a spear on the left side; but, thanks to God, we have regained strength. Know also that by twenty days after Christmas we hope, through God's grace, to receive the Holy City of Jerusalem and the Lord's Sepulchre, after which we shall return to our own land.

Witness our own [hand] at Joppa, 1st Oct.

III. The King rescues a party of foragers: 6 November 1191

A foraging party was attacked by a group of Saracen horsemen, whereupon Richard sent some knights to rescue them, promising to follow with more men as soon as he was ready. As the knights reached the foragers many more enemy horsemen appeared in what was a classic Saracen entrapment. Seeing this, some of his own men tried to prevent the king from attacking, telling him that they should not start something they would not be able to win, since they were so heavily outnumbered. As it was quite clear that the fate of the foragers and their rescuers was already sealed, one of his attendants asked Richard if it would not be the lesser of two evils that those few men should be killed rather than that he, upon whom so much depended, should be lost in a futile attack?

At this, Richard changed colour (always a dangerous sign) and snapped at him:

> When I sent my loved comrades out to war it was with the promise of bringing them aid. And if I fail to do this, so far as I can, I shall deceive those who trusted me. And should they meet with death in my absence – which I pray may never happen – never more will I bear the name of king.

With that he spurred his steed, lowered his lance and charged into the middle of the Turks.

IV. King Richard gives his reasons for not persisting with the advance to Jerusalem ca. 22 June 1192

You will not find me leading the people in such a way as to lay myself open to reprehension or shame. Truly it would be the mark of an unwary man if I were to lend myself to any such folly. But, if you see fit to attack Jerusalem, I will not desert you; I will be your comrade though not your lord; I will follow but I will not lead. Saladin knows everything that is done in our army, he knows our capacity and our strength. We are far off from the coast, and if Saladin should come down into the plain of Ramla with his host and cut off our provisions by guarding the ways,[18] would not this, I ask you, be our utter ruin? Then, however, it would be too late for repentance. Besides, the circuit [i.e. circumference] of Jerusalem, so far as we hear, is very large and if our little host were to attempt to close it in on every side, our numbers would not suffice for the siege and the protection of those who bring up our stores. Besides, if I were to sanction any such imprudence while I was leader, and if any misfortune befell us, I alone should be charged with rashness, and be reckoned responsible for the danger of all. Moreover I know for certain that there are some here (and in France too) who are most eager for me to act rashly, and lay myself open to some dishonouring charge. For these reasons I do not think fit to show any hurry in the conduct of such difficult affairs. Besides we and our people are strangers, entirely ignorant of the district, its roads and its passes ... Therefore I think it better to proceed on the advice of the natives[19] who, we may be sure, are eager to get back their old possessions, and who know the country. It seems fit to follow the advice of the Templars and the Hospitallers – as to whether we shall advance to the siege of Jerusalem or to [be]siege Babylon [Cairo], Beirut, or Damascus. If we adopt their advice our army will no longer be, as it now is, torn apart by such great dissensions.

V. Cyprus

The English Crusaders in Cyprus found themselves facing a large crowd of Cypriot troops (whom they called Griffons). The Crusaders were so greatly outnumbered that a clerk-in-arms named Hugo de Mara, went to the king and told him, 'My lord the king, it would appear to be a wise plan to decline for a time so large and so powerful a multitude.' The king answered, 'Sir clerk, as for our professions, you had better employ yourself in writing and leave war to us ...'.

VI. During the Battle of Jaffa

When the Crusaders overran the site of Saladin's camp the night before the Battle of Jaffa, Richard met a number of senior Saracens to whom he chatted 'in tones sometimes serious and sometimes jesting':

This Sultan [i.e. Saladin] is truly a wonderful man. Islam has never had on this earth a sovereign greater or more powerful than he. How then is it that my arrival has frightened him away? By God! I am not come here with my armour on and with the intention of fighting; see, I am wearing only ship-shoes instead of proper boots. Why then have you gone off?

Then he went on:

By the great God, I thought he would fail to take Jaffa in two months, and there he has taken it in two days!

Turning to Abu Bekr, he said:

Salute the Sultan on my part and tell him that I beg him in God's name to grant me the peace I ask for. It is absolutely necessary to put an end to all this; my country beyond the sea is in a very bad state. It advantages neither myself nor you that things should continue in this state.

The Rulers of the Kingdom of Jerusalem: 1099–1192

Accession	King	Grounds for accession
1099	Godfrey of Bouillon (1058–1100)	Elected by college of nobles as Lord of Jerusalem; refused title of king.
1100	Baldwin I (d. 1118)	Brother of Godfrey; took the title of King of Jerusalem.
1118	Baldwin II (d. 1131)	Cousin of Baldwin I.
1131	Fulk of Anjou (1090–1143)	Husband of Baldwin II's daughter Mélisende.
1143	Baldwin III (1130–62)	First son of Fulk and Melisende; Queen Mélisende regent 1143–52.
1163	Amalric I (1137–74)	Second son of Fulk and Mélisende. Brother of Baldwin III.
1174	Baldwin IV (1161–85)	Son of Amalric I and Agnes de Courtenay.
1185	Baldwin V (1177–86)	Son of Baldwin IV's sister Sibylla and her first husband, William of Montferrat. Count Raymond of Tripoli appointed regent.
1186	Guy of Lusignan (d. 1194)	Second husband of Sibylla, who died in 1190. Guy was deposed in 1192.
1192	Marquess Conrad of Montferrat (d. 1192)	Second husband of Isabella, daughter of Amalric I and Maria Comnena, and Sibylla's half-sister. Appointed king, but assassinated within days and never crowned.
1192	Count Henry of Champagne (d. 1195)	Third husband of Isabella, daughter of Amalric I and Maria Comnena. Never crowned.

Conversion Table

1 inch = 25.4 millimetres
1 foot = 0.3048 metre
1 mile = 1.609 kilometres

1 ounce = 28.35 grams
1 pound = 0.4536 kilogram

1 gallon = 4.546 litres
1 pint = 0.568 litre

Notes to the Text

1 A technique described in Vegetius's *De Re Militari*, which Richard carried with him.

2 A buss had thirty oars, plus a single mast and square sail (see page 154).

3 It is a curious footnote to history that she is the only Queen of England never to have set foot on English soil.

4 Isaac regained his freedom in 1194, but died the following year. His daughter, generally referred to as the 'Maid of Cyprus', is known to have been committed by Richard to the care of Queen Berengaria 'to bring her up and educate her', and the two women returned to Europe together after the Crusade.

5 Richard subsequently sold the island to the Templars for 100,000 dinars, but they resold it back to Richard who later transferred it at the same price to Guy of Lusignan, whose descendants ruled Cyprus for 200 years.

6 It was used for the disposal of animal carcasses, hence its name.

7 In March 1799, the (then) General Bonaparte invaded Syria and, following the French capture of the city of Jaffa, his troops formed a huge square inside which they slaughtered the entire Arab garrison, a total of some 3,800 men, women and children. Whether this was a conscious repeat of what happened at Acre 600 years earlier has never been adequately explained.

8 A possible size of the army on the march from Acre to Jaffa is discussed in more detail in Chapter 12.

9 A very similar situation occurred at the Battle of Minden (1 August 1759) where, due to a misunderstanding, the English infantry emerged from the line to attack the French cavalry. The commander -in-chief, Duke Ferdinand of Brunswick, lost no time in recriminations or corrections and ordered the remainder of the army to advance as well.

10 The expression 'old man' was a description of his wisdom and leadership rather than of his age.

11 He was never crowned.

12 The Crusaders always referred to Cairo as Babylon.

13 See Appendix B, page 201, for the original text.

14 Richard's practice of issuing blood-curdling threats is discussed in Chapter 9.

15 For reasons not recorded in any of the chronicles, he was never crowned king, although he was always addressed and treated as such.

16 The choice was King Amalric of Cyprus, who became this much-married lady's fourth husband. He took the title of King Amalric II of Jerusalem, while retaining his separate title of King Amalric I of Cyprus.

17 A number of maxims which refer specifically to types of formation to be used under particular tactical circumstances have been omitted.

18 Thus, preventing provisions being brought up to Beit-Nuba by way of Jaffa and Ramla.

19 i.e. the Crusaders domiciled in Outremer.

Bibliography

Books

Appleby, J.T. (ed), *The Chronicle of Richard of Devizes at the time of King Richard the First*, Thomas Nelson and Sons, London, 1963.

Archer, T.A., *The Crusade of Richard I*, David Nutt, London, 1888.

Bahā' al-Dīn Ibn Shaddād, *The Rare and Excellent History of Saladin*, trans. D.S. Richards, Ashgate, Aldershot, 2001.

Bahā' al-Dīn Ibn Shaddād and Yusuf ibn Rafi, *The Life of Saladin. By Beha ed-Din (1137–1193 A.D.)*, trans. C.W. Wilson, Library of the Palestine Pilgrims' Text Society, London, 1897.

Beeler, J.H., *Warfare in Feudal Europe: 730–1200*, Cornell University Press, London, 1972.

Bingham, Caroline, *The Crowned Lions: the Early Plantagenet Kings*, David & Charles, London, 1978.

Bridge, A., *Richard the Lionheart*, Grafton, London, 1989.

Fenwick, K. (ed), *The Third Crusade: An Eye-witness Account of the*

Campaigns of Richard Coeur de Lion in Cyprus and the Holy Land, Folio Society, London, 1958.

France, John, *Western Warfare in the Age of the Crusades: 1000–1300*, Cornell University Press, Ithaca, 1999.

Gabrieli, F., *Arab Historians of the Crusades*, Routledge & Keegan, London, 1969.

Gillingham, J., *Richard Coeur de Lion: Kingship, Chivalry and War in the Twelfth Century*, Hambledon Press, London, 1994.

Hallam, Elizabeth, *Chronicles of the Crusades: Eyewitness Accounts of the Wars between Christianity and Islam*, Weidenfeld & Nicolson, London, 1989.

Hyland, Ann, *The Medieval Warhorse: From Byzantium to the Crusades*, Combined Books, Sutton, Stroud, 1994.

Jefferey, G., *Cyprus Under an English King*, Zeno, London, 1973.

Nicholas, Sir Nicholas H., *A History of the Royal Navy*, vol 1, London, 1847.

Norgate, Kate, *Richard the Lion Heart*, Macmillan, London, 1924.

Oldenbourg, Zoé, *The Crusades*, trans. Anne Carter, Weidenfeld & Nicolson, London, 1963.

Oman, C.W.C., *A History of the Art of Warfare in the Middle Ages*, vol 1, Methuen, London, 1924.

Partington, Professor J.R., *A History of the Greek Fire and Gunpowder*, Heffer, Cambridge 1960.

Pryor, John H., *Geography, Technology and War: Studies in the Maritime History of the Mediterranean, 649–1571*, Cambridge University Press, Cambridge, 1988.

Richard of Devizes, *Chronicles of the Crusades: being contemporary narratives of the crusade of Richard Coeur de Lion by Richard of Devizes and Geoffrey de Vinsauf, and of the Crusade of St. Louis, by Lord John de Joinville*, H. G. Bohn, London, 1848; reissued AMS, New York, 1969.

Riley-Smith, Jonathan (ed), *The Oxford Illustrated History of the Crusades*, Oxford University Press, Oxford, 1995.

Riley-Smith, Louise and Jonathan, *Crusades: Idea and Reality 1095–1274. Documents of Medieval History, 4*, Edward Arnold, London, 1981.

Rodger, N.A.M., *The Safeguard of the Sea: A Naval History of Britain*, vol 1, Harper Collins, London, 1997.

Rogers, Randall, *Latin Siege Warfare in the Twelfth Century*, Oxford University Press, Oxford, 1992.

Runciman, Steven, *A History of the Crusades*, The Folio Society, London, 1994.

Seward, Desmond, *The Monks of War*, Folio Society, London, 2000.

Smail, R.C., *Crusading Warfare 1097–1193*, Cambridge University Press, Cambridge, 1995.

Vegetius, Flavius Renatus, *The Military Insititutions of the Romans (De Re Militari)*, trans. Lieutenant John Clark, London, 1767, in *Roots of Strategy*, BGen T.R. Phillips (ed), Military Service Publishing Co, Harrisburg, 1940.

Verbruggen, J.F., *The Art of Warfare in Western Europe during the Middle Ages*, Boydell Press, Woodbridge, 1997.

Magazine Articles

The Transportation of Horses by Sea during the Era of the Crusades, J.H. Pryor, *Mariners' Mirror*, Volume 68 (1982).

The Naval Architecture of Crusader Transport Ships, J.H. Pryor, *Mariners' Mirror*, Volume 70 (1984).

The Naval Architecture of Crusader Transport Ships Revisited, J.H. Pryor, *Mariners' Mirror*, Volume 76 (1990).

Index